Women and the Invention of the American Anthropology

Women and the Invention of American Anthropology

Nancy Oestreich Lurie

WAVELAND
PRESS, INC.
Prospect Heights, Illinois

For information about this book, write or call:
Waveland Press, Inc.
P.O. Box 400
Prospect Heights, Illinois 60070
847/634-0081

Preface 1999

When this essay appeared under the title "Women in Early American Anthropology" in 1966,[1] I made clear in the first footnote that it was exploratory rather than definitive and expressed the hope that it would stimulate full-scale biographies of the pioneering spirits discussed: Erminnie Platt Smith, Alice Fletcher, Matilda Stevenson, Zelia Nuttall,[2] Frances Densmore, and Elsie Clews Parsons. While I am gratified that my overall assessment of the role of women in the formative years of American anthropology has held up well enough to warrant republication, to date, only Fletcher[3] and Parsons[4] have become subjects of book-length studies.

Additional information is now available, however, on all of the women I discuss and many others as well in *Women Anthropologists* (1988) edited by Ute Gacs, Aisha Khan, Jerrie McIntyre, and Ruth Weinberg.[5] The 58 brief biographies of women anthropologists by both women and some men anthropologists cite published and archival sources for further study as well as selected works by the women whose lives are featured. The alphabetically listed biographies are cross-referenced in appendices in regard to the women's geographical areas of concentration and chronologically by age of birth, ending with women born up through the year 1934.

Kahn's Introduction (xiii-xviii) explains how the volume developed out of the editors' "experiences as undergraduate students during the florescence of the women's movement in the 1970s" and lists the topics that the various contributors were asked to give special consideration for comparative purposes. Of particular interest is attention to friendships and scholarly interactions among the women whose lives are reviewed. While providing some overall generalizations, Kahn and her co-editors see the biographies and bibliographies as "suggestions of how anthropology as a discipline has shaped and been shaped by its sizable female membership" and as a point of departure in pursuing questions regarding women's studies and the history of anthropology and anthropological theory.

I confined my accounts to women who were involved in the formative years of anthropology, cutting off my list with Parsons who was born in 1885, the year the Women's Anthropological Society was founded. By the time Parsons became interested in anthropology, after having completed a bachelor's degree in sociology some years earlier, it had become an academically taught and institutionally organized discipline. Gacs et al., whose concerns go beyond American anthropology, include Sara Yorke Stevenson (1847–1921) to whom I only advert briefly because she did not engage in fieldwork and her interests were in classical archeology. Their early women also include Ruth Underhill whom I neglected entirely although she was born two years before Parsons. I should at least have mentioned her, although, like Parsons, she was not self-taught like the earlier women (and men) and did not discover anthropology until her later years, completing her Ph.D. at Columbia at the age of 54. For all that, like Parsons, she qualifies as a woman groundbreaker for her work in applied anthropology before it was recognized as a legitimate field of endeavor and for her pioneering studies of women's roles.

Dr. Ruth M. Underhill.

It just never occurred to me when I set out to discuss the careers of early women that Underhill was *so old*. Parsons died in 1941, my freshman year in college, but I got to know Underhill in 1948 when I was starting work on my Ph.D. She had retired from government service with the Bureau of Indian Affairs and had begun a new career, teaching at the University of Denver. White haired though she was, she was worldly and fun with a trim figure and a sense of style, and very up-to-date as an anthropologist. We kept in touch through occasional correspondence and socializing at anthropology meetings. In 1960, still going strong, Underhill kindly agreed to write the preface to my first book, *Mountain Wolf Woman* (1961), the autobiography of the sister of Crashing Thunder, whose autobiography edited by Paul Radin was a landmark in the anthropological literature and inspired other autobiographical volumes.[6] I turned to Underhill because in 1936 she had published *The Autobiography of a Papago Woman*, then long out of print and not widely known but still the only full-length life story of an American Indian woman during that time and an excellent piece of work.

I was delighted when *Papago Woman* finally was reissued in 1979 and that Underhill had agreed to add introductory and concluding information about her own career as an anthropologist, recollections of her first fieldwork that had begun with the Papago, and her analytical assessment of the changes in Papago life that she had observed over more than 40 years.[7] This fine publication remains available as a Waveland Press, Inc. reprint (Prospect Heights, Illinois, 1985).

In April of 1984, as president of the American Anthropological Association, I had the privilege of presenting Underhill with a special citation of merit from the association on the occasion of her one hundredth birthday. Frail but alert, she declared it "splendid." She actually was one hundred and one! An erroneous birthdate of 1884 had been widely printed in biographical references. She died in August of 1984.

Finally, a small but historically telling commentary on the 1966 publication "Women in Early American Anthropology"— a time of transition in literary usage with regard to female names—reflecting the drive for gender equality. Traditionally, the first mention of a man included his full name and thereafter only the surname; after the first citation of a woman by her full name, subsequent mention by surname was preceded by Miss or Mrs., supposedly a mark of respect, but to feminists it was a put-down. June Helm, editor of the volume in which my essay appeared, and I favored the usage long established for men's names, but the editorial policy of the University of Washington Press, which published the book, was still committed in theory to the older form but apparently loosening up in practice. Both kinds of second mention usage and even first names alone are intermingled in the biographies.

References

1. "Women in Early American Anthropology" was first published in a volume of essays edited by June Helm for the American Ethnological Society, *Pioneers of American Anthropology: The Uses of Biography* (Seattle, University of Washington Press, 1966).

2. Among the essays in the volume cited above, "Glimpses of a Friendship" by Ross Parmenter, presents further information on Zelia Nuttall in relation to correspondence from 1901 to 1928 between Nuttall and Franz Boas, covering the period of Boas's rising recognition as a scholar and Nuttall's waning prominence.

3. *A Stranger in Her Native Land: Alice Fletcher and the American Indians* by Joan T. Mark (Lincoln, University of Nebraska Press, 1988) is an outstanding biographical volume and sheds special light on Fletcher's early years before she became interested in anthropology. Also of interest is Jane E. Gay's *With the Nez Perces: Alice Fletcher in the Field, 1889–1892,* edited with an introduction by Frederick E. Hoxie and Joan T. Mark (Lincoln, University of Nebraska Press, 1981). Gay details with humor and literary flair

Fletcher's day-by-day experiences as the allotting agent to the Nez Perces and her own role as photographer, cook, and general camp factotum to "Her Majesty, Queen Alice."

4. *A Woman's Quest for Science: Portrait of Anthropologist Elsie Clews Parsons* by Peter H. Hare, Parsons' nephew, offers rare familial recollections of a public person (Buffalo, Prometheus Books, 1985). Rosemary Lévy Zumwalt's *Wealth and Rebellion: Elsie Clews Parsons, Anthropologist and Folklorist* (Urbana, University of Illinois Press, 1992) and Desley Deacon's *Elsie Clews Parsons: Inventing Modern Life* (Chicago, University of Chicago Press, 1997) provide both personal and intellectual biographical data on Parsons' development and significance as a scholar.

5. Gacs, Ute, Aisha Khan, Jerrie McIntyre, and Ruth Weinberg, eds. *Women Anthropologists: Selected Biographies* (Westport, Connecticut, Greenwood Press, 1988; reprinted Urbana, University of Illinois Press, 1989). See also Babcock, Barbara A. and Nancy J. Parezo, *Daughters of the Desert: Women Anthropologists in the Southwest, 1880–1980* (Tucson, University of Arizona, 1986). These brief biographical sketches and selected bibliographies were prepared in connection with a 1986 exhibit, *Daughters of the Desert*, at the Arizona State Museum. They cover several women born prior to 1885 whom I did not include in my study because their work was tangential to the development of anthropology as a discipline and concentrated on the fields of art, literature, and popular anthropology.

6. In 1920, Paul Radin published "The Autobiography of an American Indian" (*University of California Publications in Archaeology and Ethnology,* XVI:381-473) and an expanded version in 1926 (New York) under the title, *Crashing Thunder,* which inspired the collection and publication of a number of highly touted autobiographical accounts of Indian men, beginning with Walter Dyk's *Son of Old Man Hat* (New York, 1938), a Navajo Indian's story.

7. Lurie, Nancy Oestreich. "A Papago Woman and A Woman Anthropologist," an essay review of the 1979 (New York) edition of Underhill's *Autobiography of a Papago Woman, Reviews in Anthropology,* Vol. 7, No. 1, Winter 1980:119–129.

About the Author

Nancy Oestreich Lurie has studied among the Dogrib Indians of Canada and a number of American Indian groups in the United States, particularly the Ho-Chunk (Winnebago) of Wisconsin and Nebraska. After completing her B.A. at the University of Wisconsin (1945) she obtained a master's degree at the University of Chicago (1947) and a Ph.D. at Northwestern University (1952). Her career has included serving as an expert witness for tribes before the U.S. Indian Claims Commission. She has taught at the University of Michigan, the University of Wisconsin-Milwaukee and, as a Fulbright lecturer (1965-1966), at the University of Aarhus, Denmark. From 1972 until her retirement in 1992 she headed the anthropology section at the Milwaukee Public Museum. She was president of the American Anthropological Association in 1983 and 1984. Her publications deal with various aspects of anthropology, including ethnohistory and applied anthropology, American Indians, and the museum field.

In choosing to write about a select group in a relatively new discipline, it is necessary to set the ground rules regarding period, persons, and problem. The problem, in the form of many engaging questions to be answered, emerged from the data which at first were collected somewhat at random. As to period and persons, the limitations are these: "early" begins with the first woman to take her place among her male contemporaries in helping to establish a recognized discipline of anthropology and ends with the termination in death of the careers of women born prior to 1885. The roster thus includes Erminnie Smith, Alice Fletcher, Matilda Stevenson, Zelia Nuttall, Frances Densmore, and Elsie Clews Parsons. The year 1885 was chosen as a significant one because it marked the founding of the Women's Anthropological Society, while the entire period under discussion reaches from the era of largely self-trained scholars who often financed their own researches to the now established arrangements of graduate training leading to the Ph.D. degree and the earning of one's living as an anthropologist. The problem is to examine and assess the early role and achievements of women in American anthropology. The following pages will concentrate on those women who attained significant professional recognition in anthropology. I have excluded, reluctantly but necessarily for purposes of comparison, that early company of women active almost entirely in the fields of folklore and classical archeology because their work is not in the main line of historical development of the discipline of anthropology as we know it today in the United States.

Before research was actually begun, a number of ideas were entertained concerning women as a group worth special attention in the history of anthropology. First, there was the somewhat sentimental motivation to rescue from obscurity women who must have been remarkable personalities if only as pioneer spirits. Second, there was the hope of excitement: militant feminism on the march doing battle for women's rights in science. Finally, there was curiosity about any definable role of women in anthropology. As it turned out, early women have been relegated to no more obscurity than have many of their male contemporaries who were also remarkable pioneer spirits. That they were unusual, given the social position of women in the late nineteenth and early twentieth centuries, is reflected in their lives, and a great deal of charming folklore attaches to their memories whenever their names are mentioned.[1] Although women in Washington, D.C. banded together in their own society for a few years as a reaction to exclusion from male discussions in that city, no woman in anthropology has ever had the struggle of an Elizabeth Blackwell in medicine[2] or a Myra Colby Bradwell in law.[3] In the United States, a generally more tolerant view has been taken toward women in the sciences than in the professions. This may be due in part to the tremendous influence in the second half of the nineteenth century of Louis Agassiz who popularized science and welcomed women to his public lectures and later to his classes at Penikese Island.[4] By the time Erminnie Adele Smith delivered the earliest recorded anthropological paper by a woman before a learned society in the United States, the 1879 meeting of the American Association for the Advancement of Science, three women had already presented papers before this group in chemistry and natural history the preceding year. Furthermore, women were listed as members of the A.A.A.S. as early as 1869.

Even the strong feminist inclinations of Elsie Clews Parsons antedated her introduction to anthropology and became progressively less urgent as she bent her efforts to anthropological research. The sense of struggle for equal acceptance and recognition which has been observed among women anthropologists since the writer joined their sometimes petulant ranks seems to be related to the increasing professionalism of the discipline.

For many years the anthropological field was open and there was a need for as many earnest researchers as would be willing to devote themselves to the task of rescuing from oblivion the data that seemed to be rapidly disappearing. Apparently, women did not become so acutely aware of contesting with men until the 1930's when, complicated by the fact of a national depression, the number of trained anthropologists threatened to exceed the number of salaried positions available in teaching and research. Although this circumstance is now changing, some bitterness unquestionably remains. The purpose of this paper is not to discuss the professional and economic fortunes of contemporary women anthropologists; however, the situation of the last several academic generations stands in contrast to that of the very early years of anthropology.

Doubtless, the first women anthropologists encountered the general difficulties of scholarly women whose ambitions seemed presumptuous — if not actually laughable — to many of their male contemporaries.[5] However, not only was acceptance relatively amicable, the more perceptive men in anthropology viewed the participation of women as peculiarly enriching to the new science of anthropology, specifically in ethnology.

It is generally known that Franz Boas recognized the particular contributions women could make to anthropology and welcomed women students who were willing to prove themselves capable of the standards of scholarship he exacted. Considerably earlier, however, no less a person than Edward B. Tylor admonished his male colleagues not to look askance at women who sought to share their intellectual interests. Tylor had made a tour of the far west where he visited James and Matilda Stevenson at Zuñi. In an address before the Anthropological Society of Washington in 1884 he commented of this couple:

> And one thing I particularly noticed was this, that to get at the confidence of the tribe, the man of the house, though he can do a great deal, cannot do it all. If his wife sympathizes with his work, and is able to do it, really half the work of investigation seems to fall to her, so much is to be learned through the women of the tribe which the men will not readily disclose. The experience seemed to me a lesson to anthropologists not to sound the "bull-roarer," and warn the ladies off from their proceedings, but rather to avail themselves thankfully of their help.[6]

Tylor obviously saw women's work in terms of a team of husband and wife, although by 1884 at least two women, Erminnie Smith and Alice Cunningham Fletcher, had engaged in field work on their own. Nevertheless, the Stevensons do appear to have been harbingers of a series of famous anthropological teams. One has the impression, although it has not been checked out quantitatively, that in other disciplines a Sidney and Beatrice Webb or a Charles and Mary Beard are exceptions and not the commonplace such pairs are in anthropology. Even when a wife does not have formal training in the discipline, she often becomes an "anthropologist by marriage" in contrast to spouses in even such related fields as sociology, psychology and economics, to say nothing of the natural and physical sciences.

However, "the ladies" freely interpreted on the Tylorian view and concluded that women as a group could obtain information complementary to that of men as a group. Furthermore, from the beginning there were lone investigators among the women who, like male anthropologists, collected all the data they could obtain. They did not depend heavily upon their roles as men or women, but upon the novelty value of the interested stranger, a role all field workers exploit to some extent as an acceptable excuse for concerning themselves with topics inappropriate to their sex or age among members of the group investigated.

Tylor had addressed a mixed audience, but the actual membership of the Anthropological Society of Washington was exclusively male. It would appear that the exclusion was not so much conscious as automatic, and reflected the usual organization of such groups in the national capital. The society was founded in 1879 by a small group of men who inserted a notice in a local newspaper announcing a meeting open to persons interested in forming an anthropological society. As far as records show, no women put in an appearance, nor, in the next few years, did it seem to have occurred to women to request membership in the group. Largely owing to the efforts of Matilda Stevenson, they simply started their own association.[7]

Unfortunately, little information is available concerning the Women's Anthropological Society, which remained active for about fourteen years, 1885–1899. Unless otherwise noted, all references to the group in the present discussion derive from a small pamphlet, "The Organization and Constitution of the Women's Anthropological Society," privately printed in Washington, D.C., in 1885. The admonition that women would have to demonstrate real sincerity and ability in order to be accepted as anthropologists may have underlain some of the serious determination implied in the pamphlet. The Women's Anthropological Society was to be no pink tea gathering of talkative ladies, refreshments were not to be served at meetings, and no paper was to exceed thirty minutes unless by special permission of the board of directors. The determination is also made explicit in such words as these:

> This organization has for its object: first, to open to women new fields for systematic investigation; second, to

invite their cooperation in the development of the science of anthropology.

In view of the intellectual future that appeared to be opening to women by 1885, the society invited:

> . . . all who are clear in thought, logical in mental processes, exact in expression, and earnest in the search for truth, to make contributions of ascertained and properly related facts, and thus aid in the solution of the mighty problems that make up the humanity wide science of Anthropology.

The women set forth their definition of the fields and organization of anthropology according to an outline suggested to them by Otis T. Mason. It includes terms such as "anthropogeny" and "hexicology," with the disciplines of sociology and psychology blithely subsumed as but subfields of anthropology. However, in various guises we see the now familiar physical anthropology, archeology, linguistics, ethnography and ethnology, and, of course, a strong orientation toward cultural evolution as not one theoretical approach but the very and only nature of the universe to be explored ever more fully and understood by specialized studies under the various categories listed in the outline.

The group did not imagine themselves as innovators in anthropology, but as contributors of special information which would enrich a defined discipline. They appeared willing to tackle almost anything, but they emphasized the special work they could do as women. For example, without really explaining how it was to be done except through "tact" and "scholarship," they pointed out that only women would be able to obtain really intimate information on life in the harem or the zenana. Yet, they did "not exhort [women] to *leave* their present life-conditions, but to *master* them." Study among faraway peoples was desirable, but, they asked rhetorically, "What state, what town, what household is destitute of choicest materials for our work?"

Though burning with scholarly zeal, so completely did they adopt ideas current in their day of ineffable spiritual differences between men and women that their flowing nineteenth century prose requires some twentieth century translating. *Man* means all humankind distinguished from animals, but *woman* means simply the female of the human species, *viz*: "The highly organized religious nature of woman gives her special adaptation for the study of the sublime *differentia*, by reason of which man, alone, sins, sacrifices, worships."

These women clearly accepted their role as women. Problems of "career *vs.* marriage" and complaints about disadvantages and discrimination attendant upon being a woman were to come later. Seeing themselves as capable of making special contributions to anthropology because they were women, and subscribing to views of their day that the infancy of the individual reflects the infancy of mankind, they engaged in further rhetorical questioning. In the "earliest unfoldings of thought, language, and belief, who can collect so valuable materials as can mothers?" For those unable to fulfill their expected destiny as wives and mothers, "every day of a teacher's life is a revelation." Their numbers must have included some bona fide early "career women," since they also mentioned the unique contributions physicians might make to anthropology.

Recognizing that women had long performed special services in works of charity and other endeavors of Christian benevolence, they chose to stress the need to understand social problems if such problems ever were to be alleviated. Thus they sought to analyze as well as to break bread with the "needy brother" in order that they might "chant in noble unison, 'I count *nothing* that affects humanity foreign to myself!'"

According to the pamphlet, the first president was Matilda Stevenson; vice presidents and board of directors were not yet chosen at the time of printing, and the other officers — Mrs. Emma Louise Hitchcock, Miss Sarah A. Scull, and Mrs. Mary

Parke Foster — did not achieve any great fame as anthropologists.

In 1893 a joint meeting was held with the Anthropological Society of Washington, and Zelia Nuttall delivered the principal address, "The Mexican Calendar System." Otis T. Mason, president of the men's group, presided, and Mrs. Nuttall was introduced by Alice Fletcher, president of the women's group. A second joint meeting held April 9, 1895, was a symposium on folklore and among the participants were Dr. Washington Mathews, Miss Elizabeth Boyant Johnston, and Col. Weston Flint. (If anthropological history takes little notice of Miss Johnston, it deals an equally fleeting fame to Colonel Flint.) Two more joint meetings were held in 1895 and at least one more in 1896. Likewise, in 1896, a joint meeting of all the scientific societies of Washington was conducted, and from this beginning the Washington Academy of Sciences was formed in 1898. In that same year, the Anthropological Society of Washington extended an invitation of membership to the Women's Anthropological Society. On January 3, 1899, forty-nine women were received into the Anthropological Society of Washington, presumably disbanding their own organization at that time since this is the last we hear of it. Their acceptance into the group was obviously complete, and by 1903 the president of the Anthropological Society of Washington was a woman, Alice Fletcher.[8]

Some curious circumstances seem to have contributed to the eventual merging of the two societies. The joint meeting of 1896 was held to discuss problems of housing in slum areas of Washington. In the spring of 1896, a committee of Washington citizens concerned with problems of housing had employed a special agent to conduct a house-to-house survey of an area comprising some 35 alleys and 191 dwellings. The Women's Anthropological Society was asked to co-operate in the undertaking and voted to support the agent for an additional month in order to complete the work and tabulate the results. Part of the tabulation and analysis was done by Miss Clara de Gaffenried, a special agent of the Department of Labor, and her findings were presented in a paper read before the Women's Anthropological Society on November 14, 1896. This is the only record obtained to date of what must have been but one of many papers presented before the group. Largely at the instigation of the Women's Society, the Washington Sanitary Improvement Company was formed as a result of action by the Anthropological Society of Washington, which became a stockholder in the firm set up to handle the construction of 808 low-rent dwellings. The Women's Anthropological Society was among the other contributors and remained a continuing force in the enterprise.[9] That the women could take such concrete action to further their social objectives is eminently understandable when it is noted that they exacted yearly dues of $5.00 from each member, did not fritter away their money on refreshments, apparently did no publishing, and the likelihood is that they allowed their dues to accrue interest.

Since the American Anthropological Association was founded at about the same time that women were admitted to the Washington Society, it is not surprising to find women numbered among its charter members. Not only did women enter anthropology early, but they endured; the last surviving charter member of the American Anthropological Association, a woman, H. Newell Wardell of Philadelphia, died in 1964. The American Ethnological Society made no explicit exclusion of women, but did not number women among its charter members in 1848 or for many years thereafter.[10] However, by the time it was reorganized along its present lines, women had been fully accepted into various scholarly organizations and have thus been active in the American Ethnological Society as a matter of course. The same is generally true of the now many local and specialized anthropological societies. The International Congress of Americanists early admitted female members and in 1892 the membership, listed according to country, included Caecilie Seler of Germany and Zelia Nuttall of the United States, "*aide spécial pour l'archeologie mexicaine au 'Peabody Museum of American archaeology and ethnology' de Cambridge (Mass.).*" [11] The Peabody apparently accepted without question those women who were sincerely interested in its work, and published studies by both Nuttall and Fletcher in Volume I of the now famous *Archaeological and Ethnological Papers*.

Almost as soon as women had demonstrated competency in anthropology they were called upon to take an active part in many anthropological endeavors. Alice Fletcher was in charge of Indian exhibits at the New Orleans Industrial Exposition of 1884–1885, but it pained her to see her friends represented only by crude aboriginal artifacts, and she accordingly wrote a letter which was printed to be circulated among Indians. She stressed the importance of education if Indian people were to take their rightful place beside the Whites in creating technological wonders. [12] The Chicago World's Fair of 1893 included a special Congress of Anthropology in which Fletcher, Nuttall, and Stevenson participated as well as Sarah Yorke Stevenson, an Egyptologist of some note, and Mrs. M. French-Sheldon who spoke on customs of the natives of East Africa. [13] Stevenson was assigned the task of collecting special display specimens of Indian artifacts for the Louisiana Purchase Exposition of 1904–1905, held in St. Louis, [14] and Nuttall served in an official capacity at this exposition. [15]

The lack of opposition to women in the early days of American anthropology is strikingly demonstrated in the career of Erminnie Smith who holds the honor, at least by a year or two over Alice Fletcher, of being the first woman to receive professional recognition for her work. Of special interest is the fact that Smith had already found scientific acceptance in an-

Officers of the A.A.A.S. at Ann Arbor, 1885. J.O. Dorsey, vice president of the anthropology section, is standing third from right; and Mrs. Erminnie A. Smith is seated in the front row. *Smithsonian Institution, Photo No. 44730.*

Major John Wesley Powell, first director of the Bureau of American Ethnology. *Smithsonian Institution, Photo No. 56188.*

other field before she became interested in anthropology. Her scientific work began with geology, and, according to her various biographies, she amassed one of the finest private collections of mineral specimens in the United States.[16]

Born Erminnie Platt at Marcellus, New York, in 1836, she was educated at Miss Willard's Seminary at Troy, and in 1855 married Simeon Smith. Her economic circumstances were quite favorable and she traveled widely. During one stay of four years in Europe with her two young sons she studied languages and also took a degree at the School of Mines at Freiburg.[17] Her first paper before the A.A.A.S., "Monograph on Jade," reflects an interesting combination of her long-standing concern with minerology and her new found fascination in anthropology. It details the trade and work in jade throughout the world.[18] Two years later, in 1881, she again appeared on the A.A.A.S. program and gave two papers on Iroquois language and mythology,[19] subjects that occupied her attention for the few remaining years of her life. It is probably safe to surmise that residential propinquity to the Iroquois as well as the widely known studies of Lewis Henry Morgan prompted the development of Mrs. Smith's interests.

She was probably the first woman to do anthropological field work, although biographical data are equivocal on the exact date. It is implied that she began work with a remnant Tuscarora group in Canada in 1878, but it may have been 1879, the year Matilda Stevenson first visited Zuñi. However, Erminnie Smith set out purposefully and alone, whereas Mrs. Stevenson simply accompanied her husband to Zuñi and developed her anthropological interests after getting into the field. Mrs. Smith was adopted by the Tuscarora, "having won their affection," and was named Beautiful Flower, Ka-tei-tci-tsa.[20] This charming incident, if it may be taken at face value, suggests that she was an ethnographer who understood the niceties of rapport.

In 1882, when anthropology was first designated as Section

H in the A.A.A.S., the ladies were out in force. Erminnie Smith presented three papers based on her field work among Iroquois groups; Alice Fletcher gave two papers dealing with observations among Plains tribes; and a single paper was read by Virginia K. Bowers of Newport, Kentucky, who is long since forgotten. Nothing more than the title of her paper is listed, and more's the pity because it's a humdinger: "The Bleaching of the Aryans. Was It Done By The Law of Repetition; The Accumulation of Effects?"[21] At least Virginia Bowers has the distinction of being the first woman on record to concern herself deeply with physical anthropology this early in the history of the discipline!

Mrs. Smith continued to present one or more papers at the annual meetings of the A.A.A.S. until her death in 1886. At the 1885 meeting at Ann Arbor she was the secretary of Section H, the first woman to serve as an A.A.A.S. officer. When the A.A.A.S. journal, *Science*, was founded in 1883, the first paper contributed by a woman was by Emily A. Nunn; numbers 17 and 18 of Volume I carried her two-part article on the "Naples Zoological Station."

Although Mrs. Smith did not get around to submitting an article, "Artificial Wampum," until 1885, she managed to be the first woman anthropologist to write for *Science*. In addition to taking Maj. J. W. Powell's part in a theory concerning wampum, she provided a detailed and little-appreciated account of her visit about 1884 to what must have been the last wampum manufactory catering to the fur trade.[22]

Erminnie Smith enjoys yet another "first." Her Iroquois language studies are reported by Powell in his "Director's Report" for Volume I of the *Annual Reports of the Smithsonian Institution*, then simply the Bureau of Ethnology. The *Second Annual Report* carries the first contribution by a woman to this famous series, "Myths of the Iroquois," and establishes Smith as a gifted scholar. Her work with the Bureau is detailed in Powell's

"Reports" until Volume VII when melancholy note is taken of her untimely death at her home in Jersey City.[23] Nor do her achievements end here. Utilizing a technique to be followed by Alice Fletcher, Edward Sapir and other scholars, Erminnie Smith led a "native" informant into the fold of professional anthropology. John Napoleon Brinton Hewitt, an educated, part-Tuscarora Indian, became interpreter and amanuensis to Mrs. Smith early in her work. He went on to achieve recognition for his own work, taking up Mrs. Smith's unfinished tasks with the Bureau, and pursuing research among both Iroquoian and Algonkian groups.[24] Considering Mrs. Smith's work in the short space of eight years, had she been blessed with Alice Fletcher's life span she would have doubtless contributed greatly to the development of American anthropology.

Alice Fletcher, born in 1838 and only two years Erminnie Smith's junior, like Smith entered anthropology rather late in life. Little is known of her early years except that her family background possessed a certain remarkability. Fletcher was born in Cuba during her parents' temporary residence on the island. Presumably there was some wealth since she traveled widely and eventually gave public lectures in New York on the Passion Play at Oberammergau. Perhaps this endeavor was for her support as family finances waned, for she was not wealthy when she took up the serious study of anthropology at about the age of forty.

Through the offices of F. W. Putnam of the Peabody Museum at Harvard, a special fellowship was set up by Mrs. Mary Copley Thaw of Pittsburgh in 1891 to enable Alice Fletcher to pursue her Indian studies for the rest of her life. Alice Fletcher's scientific studies of the American Indian grew out of an earlier philanthropic concern with their welfare. Even before she took up field work she was appointed by the Women's Indian Association as administrator of funds whereby small loans were made to Indians to enable them to buy their own land and build homes as a step toward acceptance and assimilation into White society. Commitment to the social philosophy implied in this benevolent endeavor was to be a dominating force for the rest of Miss Fletcher's life.[25] Though she was to become a respected scholar and an exceedingly perceptive thinker in many areas of Indian culture, her unwavering adherence to her original "solution" of the Indian problem blinded her to the persistent force of social identity among American Indian peoples and the real significance of interrelationships between economics and other aspects of culture. In the final analysis, the views she shared with many well-meaning Whites and the energy with which she particularly promulgated their legal implementation account in part for continued and increasing hardships to the present day among the people she strove so selflessly to help.[26]

Alice Fletcher's ethnographic studies, each detail faithfully recorded and checked for accuracy, are among the classics of American anthropology. Furthermore, her theoretical and historic interests ranged beyond mere collection of facts or broad ascriptions of traits and complexes to overall evolutionary speculations so common in her day. Her studies of Omaha religion carried her into comparative work among other Siouan speakers of the Plains, and, suspecting even older layers of cosmology and ritual from other sources, she turned to the Caddoans as the likely carrier of the more ancient forms. She had observed the Pawnee Hako Ceremony in the 1880's and as her awareness of problems of diffusion increased, she returned to the Pawnee and in the early 1890's recorded the ceremony.[27] An experienced field worker by this time, and sensitive to the deeper nuances of Indian religion, her account of the Hako ceremony, though reflecting the immaturity of anthropology when it was published, was for its day a model of painstaking scholarship coupled with philosophical perception. Throughout her life, however, the Omaha, her "first" tribe, remained her particular

Frederic Ward Putnam.

Alice Cunningham Fletcher.
Courtesy Smithsonian Institution,
Bureau of American Ethnology.

Alice Fletcher with Meepe and Martha. These two old Winnebago women used to pitch and keep the tent for the allotting agents in the field. The photograph was probably made sometime between 1887 and 1889. *Courtesy Smithsonian Institution, Bureau of American Ethnology.*

Alice Cunningham Fletcher. *Smithsonian Institution, Photo No. 45317.*

interest and source of closest personal associations among Indians.

By the time Alice Fletcher died in 1923, at the age of eighty-five, she was a sort of living legend in anthropology, active to the end in promoting scholarly enterprises and benevolent works. Mild of manner, entirely lacking in petty contentiousness though she was often required to take a stand on controversial issues, her determination was unswerving and her power to sway others almost charismatic. "Some of her opponents never were quite sure what quiet, deep river had just drifted along and left them stranded far from their selfish hopes. She didn't fight — any more than the snowflake and the sunbeam fight. Like them, she Just Kept On —." [28] Her cheerful obliviousness to reality as others saw it was at times exasperating, and at least one anthropologist who knew her personally remembered her only as a "dreadfully opinionated woman." [29]

In the early years when her concern with Indians pivoted entirely on their welfare, she met Thomas Henry Tibbles — experienced frontiersman, minister, journalist, and ardent worker in the cause of Indian rights. His account of the meeting gives a fascinating glimpse of Alice Fletcher at the beginning of her anthropological career, her charitable concerns, her ideas about the special role of women in anthropology, and above all, her determination.

> While we were in Boston in 1879, a lady told me that after studying ethnology for years in books and museums she now wished to visit Indian tribes in their own lodges, living as they lived and observing their daily customs her-self — especially the women's and children's ways.
> "Did you ever camp out?" I asked.
> "No, never."
> I found it hard to take her plan seriously. She, a thorough product of city life, was evidently nearing her forties. I could not imagine her leaving all her home comforts to go out to the far frontier and live among the Indians in an Indian

lodge. Still, she was so earnest that I reluctantly agreed to take her someday with our group for the trip she wished. But I gave her fair warning:

"You can't stand such a trip. You'll have to sleep on the cold ground. The food will be strange to you. You'll meet storms on the open prairie and be wet to the skin. Burning sun and wind will blister your face and hands. Long days of travelling will exhaust you. You'll have no privacy night or day. I'm sure you never can endure it."

"Yes, I can!" she insisted.[30]

On September 1, 1881, Alice Fletcher arrived at Omaha, Nebraska, and was met by Tibbles and Bright Eyes La Flesche, an educated Omaha woman who was associated in Tibbles' benevolent work and who soon became his wife. Tibbles assembled a camp outfit for the three-day trip across the prairies to the Omaha Indian Reservation. Fletcher came armed with letters from the Secretary of War, the Secretary of the Interior, the Post-Master General and many scientists, but her real arms and buckler were a surprising physical stamina for a small and seemingly delicate woman, a thorough delight in her task, and that unbreakable will. After introductions to members of the Omaha tribe, the two women, Tibbles, and an Omaha helper named Wajapa set off north the next day on a journey to the Winnebago Reservation, the Ponca settlement north of the Niobrara River comprised of removed Ponca who had returned to their old haunts, and finally to the Rosebud Sioux Reservation in South Dakota. Alice Fletcher had made an immediately favorable impression on the Omaha so that the Wajapa willingly answered her questions about his people and told her myths and stories. He also gave her a name from his own Eagle clan. Throughout his account, Tibbles does not identify Fletcher but designates her only by her Omaha name as "High Flyer."

Tibbles had not underestimated the hardships, bad weather, and inconveniences Fletcher could expect to encounter on her trip. One matter that he had not mentioned was the demands of Indian hospitality. The entire party suffered the results of having to partake of any food offered, no matter how sated they felt from a previous host's generosity. But she equably withstood all difficulties with only one instance of petulance at Wajapa's mild criticism of her skill as a camper. Wajapa went off and sulked at her sharp retort but soon they were on good terms again. However, despite his bestowal of an Indian name, and the good-natured friendliness, Alice Fletcher's final acceptance by the Omaha would hinge on more than a favorable first impression. In explaining her presence in the party to the Poncas, Tibbles overheard Wajapa saying, "She has come to see the Indians. She seems to be a very nice woman, but I haven't known her long enough to say for certain."[31]

Miss Fletcher was impressed by Tibbles, Bright Eyes, and Wajapa, and she was grateful to them. That her initiation into the rigors of field work was successful was largely due to them. Because they were knowledgeable, conversant in the several languages encountered on this first journey, and could communicate easily with her, a lady newly arrived from Boston, it apparently never occurred to her how atypical were the two Indians, or that Tibbles' philosophy of Indian administration derived not from his amazing familiarity with Indian life, but from White Christian values which he shared with her. Wajapa resolutely wore his White man's clothing as a matter of principle on the entire journey, although aware that his acceptance at Rosebud would be accompanied with far more gifts and favors had he come there in Indian dress. That the Rosebud Sioux did not think much of the stronger sentiment for White ways exhibited among the Omaha evidently did not impress Alice Fletcher as significant.[32] If any Omaha shared the views of the Sioux, they were the unacculturated folk whom Fletcher felt needed the educated leadership of such families as the White-oriented La Flesches.

Even educated Indians who remained knowledgeable bilingual informants could not see beyond solutions ready-made for them by kind-hearted Whites as is reflected in the touching obituary of Alice Fletcher written by Francis La Flesche, brother of Bright Eyes. La Flesche collaborated with Fletcher in writing the famous monograph, "The Omaha Tribe," and worked closely with her throughout her studies. He was her protege and virtually an adopted son. In time, the excellence of his work resulted in his transfer from the Department of the Interior, Bureau of Indian Affairs, to the Bureau of American Ethnology where he continued to make original contributions to the ethnographic literature on the Siouan-speaking Plains tribes.[33] La Flesche describes what happened when Alice Fletcher settled down to concentrate on work among the Omaha after her tour of reservations in Nebraska and South Dakota.

> She visited the Indians in their homes and began to make friends with them. At first, they were not disposed to talk, but after a time it occurred to one to ask: "Why are you here?" She replied: "I came to learn, if you will let me, some things about your tribal organization, social customs, tribal rites, traditions and songs. Also to see if I can help you in any way."
>
> At the suggestion of help, the faces of the Indians brightened with hope. The Indian continued: "You have come at a time when we are in distress. We have learned that the 'land paper' given us by the Great Father does not make us secure in our homes; that we could be ousted and driven to the Indian Territory as the Poncas were. We want a 'strong paper'. We are told that we can get one through an Act of Congress. Can you help us?"[34]

Alice Fletcher set about drafting the desired Act. She satisfied herself that not only was it the best thing for the Indians to be given small plots they could farm—after all, this was the view of all enlightened and sincere White friends of the Indians—but that this was what the Indians had come to recognize as their only hope. She spoke to each family head to gather proof of the Omahas' industrious devotion to their land. La Flesche states that as people came to Miss Fletcher for help, "Each one uttered the oft-repeated cry: 'I want a 'strong paper' which will make my home secure.'" Alice Fletcher worked out the details of an act whereby every adult Omaha would be allotted eighty acres to remain tax-free and held in trust by the government for a period of twenty-five years after which time adult, competent Indians would be granted fee patents and control over their holdings. Lands left over after distribution of allotments were to be sold for the benefit of the tribe to finance development of their farms. Fletcher had influential friends in Washington and through their efforts the act was pushed quickly through legislative procedures and was passed August 7, 1882. The frail-appearing ethnologist was appointed a special agent to oversee the surveying and allotment and in subsequent years performed similar work among the Winnebago and Nez Perce, who, along with many other tribes, were allotted under the Dawes Severalty Act of 1887 which was patterned after the Omaha Act.[35]

In 1910, after an absence of many years, Alice Fletcher returned to the Omaha for a brief visit. Considering her personal involvement in the Act of 1882, her assessment of results is fairly objective. She observed, ". . . the act has not been altogether evil nor has it been wholly good for the people." The Omaha were certainly far better off materially and were more cheerful than when she first knew them and it is small wonder that she viewed their future with optimism. She saw in the tendency to lease rather than to work the land nothing more than an unfortunate phase of adjustment to land ownership; it was really an indication of a major trend. Where Miss Fletcher assessed a few well-run farms as models for the general welfare, they were to prove short-lived exceptions. Finally, those items which she noted as "quaint survivals of old customs under a new guise," were really illustrative of adaptations and cultural persistence that have characterized Omaha life to the present day.[36]

In 1930, Margaret Mead spent a summer with the Omaha, the tribe disguised, but not for long, under the pseudonym, Antlers. In keeping with her desire to conceal the identity of the group, Dr. Mead does not mention Alice Fletcher by name but pays her respectful tribute by stating that the traditional life and history of White contact had been so completely recorded for the Antlers that she chose to work with this group because she would be able to devote her attentions entirely to modern conditions. Furthermore, Mead does not identify the anonymous scholar who provided so much of the excellent ethnographic data on the Omaha as also being the "well intentioned lady of missionary leanings" whose benevolent efforts resulted in the social and economic chaos Mead observed. Given "the psychology of American frontier days," Dr. Mead believed that individual ownership of land was probably the only solution philanthropic Whites could see for the Indians' economic problems attendant upon the loss of the buffalo.

> But the arrangements were none the less shortsighted and quite inadequate. . . . [The government] was giving this land to a people who had never owned land, who had no item of customary law or usage to govern their disposal of it. The Antlers had no sentiments for land beyond the vivid affection they felt for a familiar landscape and for the resting place of their dead. They witnessed with terror the eviction of the "Short Robes," [Poncas] their unhappy banishment to more barren lands and the pitiful return pilgrimage which a few of them attempted. But this was not the terror of the landowner, the man who had, for generations, regarded his own and his children's welfare as inalienably connected with certain plots of arable land; it was rather the fear of exile, of an unknown existence in an unfamiliar land.[37]

The course of events among the Omaha was paralleled on reservations throughout the country where allotment took place. First, several years of unprecedented prosperity were provided by the remaining natural resources, women's gardening and half-hearted farming with livestock, machinery, and seed supplied by sale of unallotted land. Homes, and furnishings, also derived from land sales, were new and any monies received from old annuities or farm income were used for luxuries of travel, staying in hotels, eating at restaurants, and buying expensive clothes. In time the remaining wild plant foods and game, as well as money, all began to be exhausted, but systematic farming on a large scale had never really been developed. Homes began to deteriorate, machinery broke down, livestock was sold to maintain the new standard of living, and the incredibly complicated problems of heirship began to set in.

Allotments were divided into ever-smaller and more scattered plots among heirs who, after 1900, began to increase with each generation. Leasing of Indian lands to White farmers proved the easiest solution; money, at least, could be fairly divided among the many heirs sharing interests in a given allotment. The occasional land-burdened individual, descendant of several generations of only children, could also lease his land and realize some return on his capital of acreage that exceeded his ability or inclinations to cultivate. The unwieldy bookkeeping, delays and squabbles about lease payments arising from the difficulties of assembling the names of all the heirs, and the often ridiculously small sum of lease money received by each heir created a clamor among the Indians to sell the land. The Omaha happened to have been allotted some of the richest farm land in Nebraska, but on all reservations there were usually Whites who were eager to buy Indian land and who were not above getting Indians in their debt so they would favor selling the family property. Between the time fee patents were issued and the beginning of the administration of John Collier as Commissioner of Indian Affairs in 1933, two-thirds of allotted Indian lands had passed into White ownership.[38] And so it came to pass that Fletcher's "strong paper" of individual allotments was far weaker than the tribal treaty relating to undivided lands.

It is possible that if Alice Fletcher had studied the Omaha thoroughly, as she later did, instead of plunging first into the matter of lands, she would have sought some other solution to the Indians' economic problems than the one she brought with her into her field work. She certainly recognized the "tribal tie" as an obstacle to "progress" as she defined it, and realized that the tribal organization could be attacked effectively by breaking down the communal ownership and occupation of land. Had she reviewed the situation exhaustively before taking action, she might have discovered that devastating side-effects would accompany her plan; and time might have also shown her that the pattern of diversified subsistence farming which she tried to impose on Indians was becoming increasingly impractical even to Whites with a strong agricultural tradition. On the other hand, she might never have overcome her basic predilections, although her outlook became progressively more relativistic in matters other than economics in which she had by then such an important emotional stake.

During Miss Fletcher's first visit among Indian groups, Tibbles strongly disapproved of her encouragement of Indian dancing and singing and her desire to observe ceremonies. To him such matters were part and parcel with the "savagery" from which he sought to raise the Indian.[39] Alice Fletcher was impressed by the sophistication of Indian artistic achievements and the contrast they afforded to the Indians' material culture. She accepted and went beyond the tolerant belief in the psychic unity of mankind and recognized that while she thought the White man's house superior to the skin tipi or earth lodge, Indian music deserved to be respected and perpetuated as uniquely valuable.

> I was perhaps as free from race prejudice as most students, but at the outset I was not prepared to admit what I was afterwards forced to acknowledge, — that my eyes and ears were

unconscious slaves of my previous training, — race training, if you will. . . .

It is not many years since the notion prevailed that the speech of savages was a mere jargon with an exceedingly limited vocabulary . . . but we now know . . . there can no more be a jargon in music than in speech.

The Indian is not a primitive man, nor properly a savage, but he is untutored; and yet we hear him voicing his aspirations and his loves in accordance with the same laws that are intelligently and consciously obeyed by a Wagner. . . .[40]

Only after the mistakes of forced cultural change were apparent could anthropologists as a group analyze objectively the points on which the mistakes had turned. Although Powell used the term "acculturation" in the First Annual Report of the Bureau of Ethnology, for Powell and other early scholars the effects of changes as the result of White contact were perceived only as a hindrance to ethnological reconstruction of precontact culture, not as a proper subject of anthropological inquiry into social and cultural process. To the early investigators it was an unfortunate, but total inevitability for Indian culture to disappear and for Indians to become assimilated beyond recognition in the general society of the country. The massive acquisition of material culture early in the contact between Indians and Whites suggested that the process of change occurred with remarkable speed and completeness. Many anthropologists of Alice Fletcher's era reacted at times to this conviction with field techniques that can only be described as ruthless. Their first obligation was to science and history, and if information could not be obtained by patient good nature, then cajolery, trickery, and pressure were justified.[41] Fletcher, for all her misguided benevolence, must at least be respected for regarding the welfare of the people she studied as her primary obligation. As a result she encountered little resistance to her work, collected highly secret data with relative ease, and maintained the **good** will of her informants for those who might follow after her in pursuit of scientific information.[42]

Alice Cunningham Fletcher maintained generally excellent relations with both colleagues and informants by a combination of humor, patience, total unselfishness, and lack of vindictiveness when crossed. Her small stature and seeming frailness apparently disarmed people who had no inkling of her reserves of strength. During one field trip she suffered a severe siege of "inflammatory rheumatism" which was to leave her crippled for life. As she lay on her bed of pain, her Indian friends gathered daily to cheer and console her by songs. As soon as she was able, and with a display of musical aptitude and memory that was particularly amazing in view of her painful illness, she managed to transcribe a large number of the songs she had heard.[43]

The pity is that the full force of such determination should have been thrust behind programs for Indian welfare that were tragically inappropriate to the Indians' needs. Although Fletcher's decisions and actions had unforeseen repercussions, one can only wonder if the reliability and thoroughness of her ethnography would have been so great had she not approached the Indians first as a helpful friend and then as a scientist. The Omaha wanted friends among influential White people in the hope that they could thus be saved the fate suffered by the Ponca at the hands of an unfriendly government. The Omaha were in no position to analyze or question what Fletcher proposed, it was only important that she had their welfare and devotion to their "homes" at heart and was *Doing Something* about it.

By contrast, Matilda Stevenson, who was younger than Fletcher, although her contemporary in research, was far more directly scientific in her field work, and she also obtained a great deal of valuable information. However, the Zuñi with

This sketch illustrated a newspaper article on the visit of James and Matilda Stevenson to the Hopi pueblo of Oraibi, Arizona, in 1886. *Courtesy Smithsonian Institution, Bureau of American Ethnology.*

Matilda Coxe Stevenson. *Smithsonian Institution, Photo No. 99-10109.*

Matilda Coxe Stevenson
with woman from
Taos pueblo. Taken
July 19, 1907.
*Courtesy Smithsonian
Institution, Bureau of
American Ethnology.*

Matilda Coxe Stevenson,
"full of years and dignity."
This photograph
accompanied Mrs.
Stevenson's obituary
published in the *American
Anthropologist* in 1916.

whom she first studied labored under no particular fears or anxieties for their lands. They were free to pick and choose among items of White culture which the Stevensons introduced — lamps, candles, soap, and window glass. While Stevenson never enjoyed the reverent esteem of an entire tribe, the friendships she made were intensely personal and those who called her "Washington Mother" thought of her as a real kinswoman. Furthermore, the Zuñi priests did not finally open their secret ceremonies to Matilda Stevenson out of gratitude, as the Omaha leaders welcomed Alice Fletcher, but out of respect for her intellectual ability to grasp their meaning and her sense of reverential respect which exceeded even that of some of the lay Zuñi. As time went by and the various pueblo groups began to feel the threat posed by White people, Mrs. Stevenson encountered rebuffs and resentment among peoples with whom she did not have the depth of friendship and long acquaintance that she had at Zuñi. Her own personality was such that she reacted much too aggressively and she is probably accountable for some of the hostility toward anthropologists that continues in the Southwestern pueblos.

Matilda Stevenson witnessed striking changes in the pueblos and she stressed the need for studies to be carried out before data were irrevocably lost. Doubtless this sense of urgency underlay her increasing tendency to throw rapport to the winds. Mrs. Stevenson came to conclude that Indians learned White ways all too successfully, thereby losing much that was precious and valuable which they should have cherished. She was deeply distressed by signs of crass commercialism and selfish individuality in the once generous and politely considerate people of Zuñi. Where Alice Fletcher had worked vigorously to endow the Omaha with the comfort, security, and quiet pleasures of White ruralism — gifts they were unable to appreciate — Matilda Stevenson noted with dismay that the Indians she knew best, when left to their own devices, all too readily acquired the profane values and behavior of the marketplace.

Matilda Stevenson became an anthropologist by marriage, but she outlived her husband by many years. Her work completely overshadowed James Stevenson's brief career in anthropology, a point well illustrated by the short and belated obituary of him which appears as a sort of afterthought, trailing her lengthy obituary in the *American Anthropologist*.[44]

Shortly after Matilda Evans' birth in Texas in 1850, her family moved to Washington, D.C. As was customary for people in comfortable circumstances in her day, her family sent her to a "female seminary," Miss Anable's School in Philadelphia, for the education that would prepare her for her eventual position in society. In 1872 she married James Stevenson, a geologist with the U.S. Geological Survey. With the founding of the Bureau of Ethnology, James Stevenson was added to the staff to report archeological remains and to collect specimens as he pursued geological research in the Territories. In 1879, Matilda accompanied her husband on an anthropological expedition which included Frank H. Cushing and J. K. Hillers.

The group spent six months at Zuñi; and there she discovered ethnology.[45] Her husband, an anthropologist by courtesy rather than training or primary inclination, was her teacher. Though always acknowledging her debt to him, Stevenson displayed a natural aptitude and intelligence uniquely her own. Like Mrs. Smith and Miss Fletcher, she was, in effect, self-trained. The Philadelphia-educated girl was no better prepared for the rigors of field work than the city-bred but intrepid Fletcher, as is shown in her straightforward account of her efforts to introduce soap and the washing of clothes among the Zuñi. "Never having had any experience in that work herself, she soon had most of the water from the tub on the floor and was drenched to the skin." Undaunted by invidious comparisons to the efficiency of the missionary's wife in the laundry, she persisted in her gospel of cleanliness until her work had attracted many followers.

The details of this small incident are revealing of Matilda Stevenson's ability to rise objectively and matter-of-factly above her sheltered rearing. She chose a transvestite as her first pupil in the art of washing and ironing, recognizing in Wé-wha qualifications of role and personal influence for initiating new ideas. At first, Wé-wha was considerably less than enthusiastic about the project. However, the beauty of freshly laundered clothing, enhanced by the male strength he brought to what in those days was an exhausting task, appealed to his vanity. Furthermore, he was enterprising, a trait Stevenson counted on when she selected him as her student. He soon set himself up in the laundry business for the ethnological expedition and then solicited business among other Whites in the area. His gleaming clothes served as a billboard, and before long other Zuñi were washing their clothes by Stevenson's methods. Matilda Stevenson noted with scholarly interest that they made no sex designation in the new task; men washed their own clothing, and women washed their own and their children's clothing.

Mrs. Stevenson's forthright acceptance of Wé-wha illustrates a degree of scientific and personal sophistication noteworthy for her time and her sex. She described Wé-wha as the largest of any Zuñi she knew; he was over six feet tall and muscular. Speculations by local Whites that he was a hermaphrodite seemed incorrect to her and she believed him to be physically a male, but psychologically and socially entirely female. In referring to Wé-wha, Mrs. Stevenson would employ only feminine pronouns and would not close the words in quotation marks. Her deep affection and admiration for this remarkable person were entirely those of a close and unquestioning friendship between any two women.[46]

While Erminnie Smith was being accorded rave notices by

Powell in the first volumes of the Bureau of Ethnology, Matilda Stevenson labored unheralded; and only her husband's work was mentioned in the first four "Reports" of the Director. Although she published in 1881 a thirty-five page study, *Zuñi and the Zuñians*, it was privately printed and evidently brought her little scholarly attention. Her first important recognition was bestowed by Edward Tylor in his comments about her field work, and her publication of the "Religious Life of the Zuni Child" in the *Fifth Annual Report* of the Bureau of Ethnology. She had concentrated purposefully on affairs concerning women and children in the belief that as a woman she could obtain particularly complete information, a point that figured in the philosophy of the Women's Anthropological Society founded and first presided over by Matilda Stevenson.

However, Mrs. Stevenson, being attracted to religion even in her study of children, soon concerned herself with far more than womanly matters. In 1881 she and her husband made an archeological tour of ruins in Arizona and New Mexico and visited the various Hopi villages where she made ethnological observations. James Stevenson died in 1888 at the age of forty-eight. His widow outlived him by twenty-seven years. Initially, she devoted herself to working up her husband's notes, and was accorded a staff position with the Bureau of Ethnology. In 1890 she went back alone to the field to begin work at Sia Pueblo. Although she worked at several pueblos, she returned frequently to Zuñi and by 1895 succeeded in gaining admission to heretofore forbidden rites.[47]

Perhaps childlessness and widowhood before the age of forty contributed to a self-sufficiency of attitude that came to characterize Matilda Stevenson, or perhaps she was naturally a rather humorless person. Certainly, those assessments we can make of her personality reveal a woman who insisted on being taken very seriously. W. H. Holmes, who recalled her with deep gratitude for nursing him through a critical illness while he was in the field, describes her as "able, self-reliant, and fearless, generous, helpful and self-sacrificing."[40] Admirable traits, indeed, but equally applicable to Alice Fletcher. Tibbles, however, noted Miss Fletcher's ready smile and amused laughter, and La Flesche remembered warmth and an easy friendliness.

Matilda Stevenson's sometimes overbearing disposition may have been justified in her own mind as selfless devotion to continuing her husband's work in the cause of Science. It is common knowledge that she had a low tolerance of criticism of her work, even from Major Powell with whom she argued vehemently. She herself admitted that when the "populace" — though not the priests — at Zuñi opposed her taking photographs of ceremonies and sacred paraphernalia because they feared having these things "carried away on paper," she managed to sketch everything secretly.[49] On another occasion, her insistence on obtaining data led to her being held prisoner in a kiva at the Hopi pueblo of Oraibi until she was rescued by the trader, Thomas Keams. She brought the trouble on herself; the Indians "had repeatedly warned the white people not to attend their ceremonials and to keep away as much as possible from the pueblo. . . ."[50] Actually both James and Matilda Stevenson were involved. A lurid account of the incident appeared in the *Illustrated Police News* of March 6, 1886, in which Matilda is credited with saving the day under the headline and subheading:

COWED BY A WOMAN

A CRAVEN RED DEVIL WEAKENS IN THE FACE OF A RESOLUTE WHITE HEROINE — EXCITING ADVENTURE IN AN INDIAN VILLAGE IN ARIZONA.

The reporter places the capture and threats of violence on a roof-top rather than in a kiva, and attributes the hostility of the Hopi to a generalized antipathy to White people rather than to any particular grievance against the Stevensons.

> Col. Stevenson says that while the situation was highly interesting, it was probably less alarming than it would have been to people unacquainted with the natural timidity of the Pueblos. Mrs. Stevenson who has sojourned with her husband among many wild tribes and knows the Indian character well, created an opportune diversion by shaking her fist in the face of a hunchbacked savage, whose vindictive eloquence seemed to exert a most mischievous influence over his fellows, addressing to him at the same time several brief but vigorous remarks in English and Spanish, which he was, of course, quite unable to understand. Before the man had recovered his self-possession, the strangers had backed down the ladders, and then slowly made their way, with the whole howling pack — men and women, children and dogs — at their heels, to their ponies, mounted and rode down to camp.

Meanwhile, the article explains, word of the disturbance had reached Keams who rode out with a rescue party and, finding the Stevensons safe, captured the Hopi leaders and held them prisoner at his camp for four days, threatening more dire action should they repeat such behavior as their treatment of the Stevensons.

Matthew W. Stirling notes that although Matilda Stevenson had died in 1915, when he first came to Washington in 1921 she was still a "lively legend."

> *When I became Chief of the Bureau in 1928, I inherited the office secretary of my predecessor, J. W. Fewkes. This was May S. Clark, who as a young woman had worked with Tilly at Sia in the 1880's.*
>
> *During the several years that she worked for me, Miss Clark related to me a number of Stevenson anecdotes.*
>
> *Because she wanted her hands free for note taking and did not otherwise wish to be interrupted in making ethnologic observations, Tilly turned over her camera to Miss Clark, who made the photographs illustrating the Sia report (11th Ann. Report BAE). She had*

never taken a picture before. The [photographs of] interiors of kivas etc. were [made by] flashlight, many of which later had to be retouched or redrawn by an artist.

When Miss Clark arrived at Sia, Mrs. Stevenson had preceded her. On the day she reported, Tilly told her that an important kiva ceremony was being held and that they would attend it and make notes and pictures. It was here that Tilly handed over the camera and informed May that she was the photographer. Miss Clark protested that she did not know how. Tilly said: "Never mind that, I'll show you!" — which she proceeded to do. They went to the kiva where there was a guard by the ladder at the entrance. He protested that they could not go in. "Never mind him" said Tilly, "Go on down. I will follow you." Frightened half to death, May, clutching her camera in one hand and her skirts in the other, entered the dark and smoky chamber; Tilly right behind her. They sat in a vacant spot against the wall until their eyes adjusted to the darkness. The no doubt horrified participants in the ceremony sat sullenly and stopped completely whatever they were doing. They refused to move and finally after a half hour wait, Tilly gave up and left.

After this bad start, it took a lot of tact and the intervention of the agent before she began to get cooperation. However, Tilly was nothing if not persistent and eventually she did get access to a number of kivas and permission to record the ceremonies, apparently at the same time getting the respect of the Indians who admired her obvious fearlessness.

Leslie White has commented that Matilda Stevenson's sense of self-importance took some curious forms. He had seen the original photograph of a Sia altar in the Stevenson materials at the Bureau of American Ethnology and noted that along with clearly aboriginal objects there were two small ceramic dogs of Chinese origin. When a hand-drawn copy was made for reproduction of the photograph in Stevenson's Sia study, she had simply had the dogs deleted without comment.

Nevertheless, for all her personal idiosyncracies, Matilda Stevenson's relationships with the Zuñi were decidedly cordial and her admiration for the people and their ways both sincere and affectionate. It should be remembered that the Zuñi met her as a young woman, still admittedly capable of making mistakes but eager to learn. There was also the softening influence of her husband to whom she was deeply devoted. During her married years she often signed herself as "Tilly," even in publications, and not until later did she consistently use the more dignified "Matilda." More than any other portrait of early women in anthropology, the studio photograph of Stevenson that accompanies her obituary reveals the person and her devotion to her work. She is shown full of years and dignity, a stern, matronly woman with white hair carefully coifed, pince nez glasses adding to the severity of her facial expression. But on the magnificent and elegantly garbed bosom resposes, gaudy and incongruous, a clankingly enormous squash blossom necklace.

The bibliography accompanying her obituary sets forth the varied and yet limited nature of her interests. She wrote of the need for overall, coordinated studies of the pueblo groups, but her own researches were fragmented and scattered — ranging among legends and irrigation ditches, games and ethnobotany, with a strong emphasis on the study of religious matters. She collected facts, set them forth precisely and in detail, and analyzed them largely within their own context. Her works, particularly on Zuñi, remain standard references for any student of the Southwest. It was left for later scholars to assess broader meanings and develop wider, interpueblo conceptualizations.

Like Alice Fletcher, Matilda Stevenson was able to return at intervals to her "first love," and after a period of twenty-five years she reported on changes that had occurred among the Zuñi. Where Fletcher's later observations of the Omaha pictured the people on the road to a better life in their adaptations to White ways, with perhaps a few unfortunate consequences, Stevenson was appalled to discover:

. . . great strides have been made in certain directions; but in 1904 the people were found to be in a deplorable moral condition. . . .

The general improvement in living is due principally to additional trading stations scattered through the country. The adoption of foreign ways, however, has brought with it, the evils of intoxication and trickery in dealing with the white man whom they delight to lie to and cheat, though among themselves the Zunis are still honest.

. . . but alas, the Zuni as a man and a good citizen has fallen far below what he was before he came into contact with the White man. In 1879 no amount of money would have purchased a genuine Zuni mask, and not for the world would they have manufactured a bogus specimen. . . . At present the less orthodox men will manufacture almost anything a collector may desire and spurious ancient fetishes are made by the sackful and passed off as genuine.[52]

Despite her introduction of the use of soap to the Zuñi in 1879, Mrs. Stevenson was not so impressed with the greater cleanliness of the village and houses in 1904 that she did not feel that as one thing might be gained a greater thing might be lost. Matilda Stevenson, always a little apart from people, nevertheless understood far better than did the fully accepted Alice Fletcher that it is the integrity of a people rather than their standard of living that makes for contentment and a deeply meaningful existence.

In the final paragraph of her major work on the Zuñi, Matilda Stevenson begged scholars to study all the pueblo groups so that local details and indications of overall relationships among them might be fully explored and understood before the information would be lost forever.

For this work the passing hours are golden, for not only are the villages losing their old-time landmarks but the people themselves are changing, are adapting themselves to suddenly and profoundly altered environment; and the Zuni at least, whose religion teaches them to speak with one tongue, to be gentle to all, and to subdue the passions, thereby winning the favor of their gods, are under the influences of modern conditions, losing the restraining power of this religion, and as a result, are changing for the worse.[53]

In her last years, Mrs. Stevenson made her home near San Ildefonso where she continued her researches. To one young archeologist working in the region she was a relic of other days, and her overbearing officiousness finally caused her to appear a silly old woman to Indians and anthropologists.

> *I never cottoned much to her nor did the Indians at the pueblo, I think. Anyhow, she once told me that they called her "Little Flower" and when I passed that on to the linguist, John P. Harrington, he asked one of his San Ildefonso informants about her, telling him of the name she had given me. The Indian laughed and John asked him why. He said, "That word doesn't mean 'Little Flower,' it means 'Big Bottom!'"*[54]

It is common knowledge that as she grew older, Matilda Stevenson took increasingly to drink, but as Stirling notes, "It would probably be unfair to consider the disagreeable alcoholic of these later times as being the same person as the strong willed, able person that she was during her productive years. . . ."

Matilda Stevenson's primary failing as an ethnologist was not her aggressiveness nor her tendency to deal with isolated phenomena, but her woeful lack of a saving sense of humor. Almost any other ethnologist, even before the days of modern acculturation studies, would have welcomed those Chinese dogs on a Sia altar as a chance to inject a mildly amusing comment to relieve the pedestrian pace of ethnographic reporting. Mrs. Stevenson was outraged, and firmly removed the offending objects from view.

However, Matilda Stevenson was not the only female anthropologist in the early days to enjoy a reputation for antagonizing people, trusting in the utter verity of her own ideas. Zelia Nuttall was also notable in this regard, although Zelia con-

Photograph taken by Matilda Stevenson, in 1888 or 1889, showing the Altar of the Knife Society, pueblo of Sia, New Mexico. Note the Chinese dogs in the center of the photograph. *Smithsonian Institution, Photo No. 2190.*

Painting by M.I. Wright after Stevenson's photograph. The Chinese dogs have disappeared.

Top, left: Zelia Nuttall, dressed in the costume she wore to a ball at the Palazzo Vecchio in Florence in 1898. *Top, right:* Zelia Nuttall in 1927.

Zelia Nuttall. Photograph taken in England between 1912 and 1914.

fined her contentiousness to colleagues. This, of course, was largely a matter of opportunity since Mrs. Nuttall concentrated on archeological and ethnohistorical research rather than on ethnography. Like Matilda Stevenson, Zelia Nuttall is remembered for her personality rather than for her works. Yet, Matilda Stevenson's official obituary tells us little about the woman except that she worked hard and diligently in the cause of anthropology; we must seek her idiosyncrasies between the lines of her writing and the less formal recollections of those who knew her, or perpetuate the legends about her. However, even Tozzer's restrained memorial cannot hide the fact that Zelia Nuttall was a controversial, sometimes wrong-headed, but delightfully colorful and brilliant woman.[55] Mrs. Nuttall never felt obliged to collect data especially pertinent to her sex as did Mrs. Stevenson, at least early in her career; her applications of anthropological knowledge had no particular relationship to social welfare according to the philosophy of the Women's Anthropological Society, but Zelia Nuttall was a *woman* anthropologist. Her work might have been done by either a man or a woman, more so than some of Matilda Stevenson's work relating to children, but the zest she brought to her studies and her squabbles with her colleagues are unmistakably feminine. One is reminded of the prima ballerina or first soprano. It is a mark of anthropology having come of age that a woman entering the field could be an esteemed scholar and remembered as attractive or exasperating as a woman. As noted, Mrs. Nuttall was among the first women to represent the United States in the International Congress of Americanists. "At meetings she was the center of interest," able to speak all the major European languages, but fascinating to those gathered about her for her "majestic presence, her wit, and her knowledge."

Zelia Nuttall's role of urbane sophisticate was provided by a most unusual family background; she simply brought to it a remarkable intellect and a surprisingly disciplined scholarliness, if not a contemplative calmness, in argument.

Zelia Nuttall was born of wealthy and socially prominent parents in San Francisco, California, in 1857. Her family moved to Europe in 1865, where they spent the next nine years, and young Zelia acquired a remarkable facility in languages. Although a number of years were to pass before she actually visited Mexico, her childhood reading about the history and antiquities of that country had already sparked her archeological inclinations. In 1880 Zelia married Alphonse Louis Pinart, a French anthropologist, whose special interests were linguistics and folklore. She bore one daughter, Nadine, in 1882. But the marriage was not happy and two years lated this early, ill-starred team of anthropologists separated. Zelia resumed her maiden name and kept custody of her child after her divorce in 1888.

She made her first trip to Mexico in 1884 in company with her daughter, mother, and younger brother, and began serious study of Mexican archeology. In 1902 she returned to Mexico, after extended travels throughout the world, and made her permanent home there. Her residence, Casa Alvarado at Coyoacan, is recalled by older members of the discipline who worked in Mexico as an impressive mansion and a haven to visiting scholars, graciously presided over by a charming hostess.

One bit of folklore is so revealing of the woman and occurs so persistently when Zelia Nuttall's name is mentioned that it should be noted here in the hope that the date and participants can be identified. On one occasion, the story goes, two young archeologists paid a visit at Casa Alvarado. As they gazed about the magnificent home, their hostess, beautifully dressed with trailing skirts, started across the room to greet them. Suddenly, her drawers slithered down around her ankles but she stepped gracefully out of them without breaking stride. A maid immediately gathered up the offending garment and hastened off, and

Zelia Nuttall with unruffled aplomb greeted her guests as if the incident had never occurred.

Her first scholarly work dealt with the Mexican calendar system on which she read and published a number of papers. Her studies evoked such favorable notice that in 1886 she was appointed an honorary assistant in Mexican Archeology at the Peabody Museum of Harvard University, a rank she held for the rest of her life. She became fascinated by problems of diffusion and her largest work, "Fundamental Principles of New and Old World Civilization," was published by the Peabody in 1901. She always considered it her major opus, although the kindest judgment accorded it is Tozzer's assessment that before her death it had already become "archaic." However, the curator of the Peabody, Professor F. W. Putnam, shared Nuttall's views and was thus delighted to publish her work.

Other, less ambitious undertakings added new and important information to the study of Mexican antiquities and her position as a scholar rests on them. Mrs. Nuttall's special talent was in finding lost or forgotten manuscript materials and making them available to the scholarly world. Tozzer implies that there was something uncanny in the ability that led her to poke about in unlikely repositories in the Old and New Worlds. It would seem that if anyone could have put feminine intuition to work, it would have been the indefatigable Zelia. The "Codex Nuttall," published by the Peabody Museum immortalizes her name, and a long list of other remarkable documentary materials found publication at Nuttall's hands. However, "Mrs. Nuttall's vivid mind, independent will, and a remarkable belief in the truth of her theories caused her life to be punctuated with controversies." Her most notable altercation was with the Duc de Loubat over publication rights of the "Codex Magliabecchiano" which she had discovered at the Biblioteca Nazionale Central at Florence. She was often on the side of right, but it appears that she certainly did not hesitate to enter controversy with a zest. Perhaps the most harmless and at the same time most amusing of her efforts to gain recognition of some pet theory was her designation of a day in May as the ancient New Year's Day of the Mexicans. She worked long and hard to have the children of Mexico engage in special festivities around markers set up in village plazas for the occasion. She even entered into negotiations with several Peruvian associations in the hope of spreading the celebration of the holiday.

Although Mrs. Nuttall could take herself very seriously in what now seem silly enterprises, one of her little-known publications reflects a certain wicked playfulness characteristic of a sophisticated person. "The Causes of The Physical Degeneracy of Mexican Indians After The Spanish Conquest as Set Forth by Mexican Informants in 1580," was published in the English *Journal of Hygiene* in 1928.[56] Taken as a whole the accounts ascribe the degeneracy to more leisure, a greatly increased intake of meat, baked bread, more frequent changes of clothing, softer living, and comfortable beds; sybaritic luxuries one hardly tends to associate with the horrors of the Conquest. Nuttall, not content with simply providing documentary evidence of the dangers of civilization to readers of a scientific journal oriented toward health, comments at the outset that while she does not care to become involved in the argument, here apparently was ammunition for the vegetarian movement!

During Zelia Nuttall's later years, the large and beautiful gardens at her home in Mexico were her special pride and pleasure. She raised unusual plants and flowers and also developed an interest in the collection and identification of ethnobotanical specimens. She died at her home, Casa Alvarado, at the age of seventy-six, the "last of the great pioneers of Mexican archeology."

Another woman who pioneered in a highly specialized branch of anthropology was born ten years after Zelia Nuttall. Though her works were to be widely read, she lived out her life in such quiet obscurity that when she died in 1957, at the age of ninety, her passing was scarcely noted. By that time, most people assumed that she was long since dead if they thought of her at all. Frances Densmore was born in Red Wing, Minnesota, of old Midwest stock. Her interest and aptitude in music led her to concentrate in that field, and in due course after completing her education in public schools she went away to college at Oberlin, Ohio, where she took a degree in music. She studied under Leopold Godowsky in 1898, and achieved some recognition as a professional musician, notably in piano and organ performances.[57] However, for unknown reasons she did not stray far nor for very long from Red Wing during her early years. About 1893 she became interested in the music of the Chippewa Indians near her home. She saw a tremendous boon to comparative musicology in the invention of the phonograph, and some time after 1901 she borrowed a machine and cut wax cylinder records of a number of Chippewa songs. She sent them with notes to the Bureau of American Ethnology. They were received with enthusiastic appreciation, with the result that Frances Densmore became officially associated with the institution for the rest of her life.[58] In the succeeding years, she recorded and made notes on over 2,400 songs which now comprise the Smithsonian-Densmore Collection. Stirling recalls Densmore as "a very methodical person."

> *Every year she made an appointment to see me in Washington to discuss her field work for the coming year. The Bureau had an annual Government appropriation "For the Study of Indian Music" to the amount of $3000. Since she had no salary, this money was essential to the conduct of her work, which she carried on in a most economical manner. She had a feeling of insecurity about the continuation of this fund, and I felt sure that the primary purpose of her visits to me was to reassure herself that the money would be available each year, since Government funds could not be committed more than a year in advance.*

She told me that she had been advised by Dr. Walter Hough never to read any scientific reports in advance on the people she was to visit, since these might inadvertently influence her interpretations. She took this advice very seriously, and one may be sure that her ethnological interpretations are her own.[59]

Miss Densmore's career spanned the entire development of mechanical recording equipment from cylinders to tape. Her work took her to all the major culture areas of North America on visits to dozens of different tribes where she recorded music and gathered a wealth of related ethnographic material which she incorporated into her discussions of music, including a greater amount of good photographic illustration than can be found in many standard ethnological monographs. She also collected herbs used in connection with various healing songs and ceremonies.[60]

A cousin who knew her well provides the following personal assessment of Frances Densmore:

. . . she was very pleasant and interesting in conversation, always abreast of the times, had a keen sense of humor, and enjoyed her circle of friends — but she had no interest whatever in social life. From the time she took up this work it was her one consuming interest and nothing was allowed to interfere or detract from it. From her early days, all through the more than fifty years with the Smithsonian, until her death . . . she lived and labored solely for this great interest.[61]

Although she gave her life over entirely to her work, Frances Densmore lived long enough to escape the sense of urgency that would lead to haste and antagonizing of informants. Her publications reveal an easy relationship with Indian people and respect for them as individuals. She took her acceptance so much for granted that in explaining how she obtained the songs she simply stated in one publication that "Care is taken in selecting the singers and in explaining to them the nature of the material desired, and effort is made to free them from constraint or embarrassment, in order that the recorded song may be free and natural." [62]

She attained linguistic competency and ethnographic skill as essentials to further her musical analyses, and she matured quickly as a scholar and a scientist. One of her early publications, written shortly after her work had begun in earnest with American Indians, concerned a visit with the Philippine peoples resident at the Louisiana Purchase Exposition of 1904. On the basis of comparisons between Philippine and North American Indian music she presented a fine-spun and naïvely evolutionary analysis of the origin and development of music in four stages. It is very obvious that the most exciting part about this work was the people rather than their music. The affable smiles of known headhunters made her "shiver," and she was delightedly terrified at the wild clashing of shields and mock fighting that accompanied Moro music. However, in her wry comments on this choreographic production we see a charming person who could be nothing but a good ethnographer: "I was told that this too was an improvised love song, and I infer that the course of true love in Mindanao is indeed strenuous." [63]

By the time her two-volume study of Chippewa music appeared, the dedicated ethnomusicologist was concerned with the detailed theoretical analysis of non-European music, its meaning in its own cultural setting, methods of making valid written transcriptions, and the historic and social significance of given songs. Throughout Frances Densmore's long life she traveled from one Indian group to another, constantly refining her techniques of recording and analysis. Her accomplishments have generally enjoyed a greater esteem in musical than in anthropological circles since few anthropologists are trained to follow the technical complexities of her highly specialized studies. She was awarded an honorary A.M. degree at her own college, Oberlin, in 1924, and the Litt. D. Degree at Macalester College in 1950. [64] Her work was used as the basis of an opera, "Winona," by Alberto Bimoni of the Juilliard School of Music; it also inspired the composer Charles W. Cadman to write compositions with Indian themes.[65] That she continued to labor in her chosen field until the end of her life is shown in the fact that the article in *Science* commemorating her ninetieth birthday reports that she had just finished reading proof on music studies of Acoma, Isleta, Cochiti, and Zuñi pueblos. Although Frances Densmore was primarily an ethnomusicologist, her ethnological acumen was great and deserves wider attention that it has generally received.

It is noteworthy that all of the women discussed thus far were self-trained in anthropological research and that none were teachers. Elsie Clews Parsons, born in 1875, is the last representative of this older group in terms of years, but her career began well after the development of formal instruction in anthropology and continued through the modern academic professionalism of the discipline. Elsie Clews, even more impressively than some of the others, was born to wealth and a high social position. But she lived in an era when such advantages no longer could be simply enjoyed by those who wished to pursue scholarly studies or who had a sense of social enlightenment. She insisted on entering the newly founded Barnard College rather than one of the older, prestigious women's schools and eventually completed graduate studies in sociology at Columbia University. She married Herbert Parsons, a prominent New York attorney and congressman, and bore six children, four of whom lived to maturity. Elsie Clews Parsons is recalled as a woman of imposing appearance, given to rather original dress; and even during her graduate career, according to Alfred Kroeber, "her statuesque figure floated through the seminar alcoves of the Low Library on Morningside Heights as a memorably astonishing sight."[66] According to several accounts of her life, she early allied herself with the cause of feminism, but fundamen-

Top, left: Portrait of Frances Densmore "wearing dress worn when giving lecture on Indian music at the Art Institute, Chicago on February 21, 1899." By Phillips, Red Wing, Minnesota. *(No. 54614-A) Top, right:* Frances Densmore, ca. 1950s. *(No. 54614-C) Below:* Main'ans or Little Wolf and Frances Densmore. Photograph by Gill, 1908. *(No. 537-B-2) All photographs Smithsonian Institution.*

Above: Elsie Clews Parsons, Southwest, ca. 1925. *Elsie Clews Parsons' Papers: Courtesy American Philosophical Society. Below, left:* Elsie Clews Parsons. *Below, right:* Franz Boas. *Smithsonian Institution, Photo No. MNH-8301.*

tally her concern was for the right to rational individual expression, unconfined by arbitrary social limitations of sex, class or race.

During the period that her children were young, she wrote extensively on social issues, particularly on the role of women and the nature of the family. Leslie Spier says these productions were "quite in the tradition of the old 'comparative ethnologist,' but saved from their curiosity-shop speciousness by her greater keenness of insight and soundness of psychology." [67] At about the age of forty Mrs. Parsons discovered anthropology as the result of a trip to the Southwest where the pueblo peoples fascinated her. Her subsequent search for guidance in the scientific study of culture brought her into contact with P. E. Goddard and Franz Boas.

By 1915 anthropology had come sufficiently of age so that empirical methods had been developed to deal with the problems Mrs. Parsons had wrestled with only philosophically in the sociology of the 1890's. In 1915 she made her first trip to Zuñi where she returned in 1917 and 1918, years during which she also made studies at Laguna. Her interest centered in the pueblo groups although she did study the Pima in Arizona, and the plains Caddo and Kiowa in Oklahoma, in seeking for pueblo relationships in a wider area. After 1929 she concentrated on Mexican groups, the Cahitans of Sonora and especially the Zapotecs of Oaxaca, the basis of her most famous study, *Mitla: Town of the Souls*, published in 1936. [68]

Mrs. Parsons managed to maintain two specializations in anthropology. In addition to her studies among Indian peoples, she also concentrated intensively on folklore of the New World Negro, collecting accounts in the vernacular and inspiring the further recording of such data by others. Interest in culture-contact problems such as her study of Mitla led her to South America. She died only a few weeks after returning from field work in the Andes. [69] Elsie Clews Parsons' work requires no special review. Still widely read, it is in the modern tradition of anthropology, concentrating on processes rather than on the simple assembling of fact.

Of particular relevance to the present study is Parsons as a historic figure. Women who preceded her in the discipline were remarkable according to type in terms of their era. Their natural intelligence coupled with relatively high social position and refinement of education allowed them to transcend the usual avocational and vocational limitations then placed on women. Elsie Clews Parsons too was a remarkable woman, but again, remarkable according to type characteristic of her era. For Parsons, it was not enough that she, as a woman, be able to achieve what she wished to do. She was concerned that no woman, really no competent person at all, be deprived of the opportunity to realize fully his intellectual potentialities.

As the other women are remembered as outstanding examples of a type of nineteenth-century personality, so too Mrs. Parsons is remembered as exceptional even in the company of many noteworthy contemporaries in the twentieth century. She came to see the cause of feminism as but part of a larger cause, the right to individual expression. Moreover, she did not confuse the pleasures of individual self-realization with meaningless symbols of achievement acquired for the sake of professional prestige. Although eager for women to be recognized for their intellectual worth, Mrs. Parsons did not feel compelled to be the standard bearer of scholarly accomplishments of her sex before the world. Her personal inclinations were such that she did not care to take on organizational offices. Since, by chance, she was independently wealthy, she was generous and recognized her obligations to other scholars. She expressed the view that official positions should be accorded to deserving and responsible people, but to people more active in academic life than she, who would find them useful in furthering their careers. Spier notes that because of her ability and in spite of her preferences, offices were "thrust upon her." Even the distinction of being the first woman president of the American Anthropological Association occurred at the end of her career and was in no way related to her earlier efforts to win equal opportunities and respect for women. She was simply elected in the due course of events as one of the most outstanding anthropologists of her time.[70]

A glance at the voluminous bibliography of Elsie Clews Parsons' writing reveals a person who must have possessed amazing reserves of energy and tremendous will. And yet, the personal recollections recorded about Parsons depict a woman characterized by great calm, relaxed sociability, and contemplative impartiality. Gladys Reichard recalled: "She used to say that her idea of complete comfort was to have *at the same time* a cigarette, a cup of coffee and an open fire."[71] One sees in Elsie Parsons something of Alice Fletcher in the affection she evoked among those who know her and in the determination and ability to follow the dictates of conscience and conviction without shrillness or loss of personal control. However, where Miss Fletcher labored largely alone and was unable to test the validity of her ideas, Mrs. Parsons, typifying a new generation of women anthropologists, had the benefit of purposeful training and wide interchange of ideas among teachers, peers, and even students. Mrs. Parsons' natural talents were shaped and refined in ways denied her predecessors.

Although Mrs. Parsons' career as a teacher was brief — a few years as a lecturer at Columbia University and a faculty position at the New School for Social Research which she helped to found — it was enriching. Parsons disliked public lecturing but she was vitally interested in the work of younger scholars. The full accounting of her financial assistance to promising students will probably never be known. While she was pleased to help further anthropology, it embarrassed her deeply to be thanked as an individual. To Elsie Clews Parsons, anthropology was a calling rather than a profession.

Where Alice Fletcher had used her anthropological influence in obtaining what she thought was best for Indians, Parsons learned to assess the dangers of trusting in expertise rather than in anthropology itself. She gave the matter a great deal of thought and it forms the basis of the presidential address which she did not live to deliver personally.[72] She viewed with horror the misuse of anthropology in the racist schemes of the Nazis, but she was also alert to the hazards attendant upon the utilization of anthropology to achieve any specific and immediate ends. When work is so directed, no matter how benevolently, "even slow and patient searches for social laws may easily smack of divination which according to our definition is concerned not with process but with particular interests and is callous to scientific control." However, continuing to reflect her fundamental concern with the individual, she saw in the data and methods of anthropology the liberation of thought whereby people may reach meaningful understandings and valid conclusions. Anthropologists, she believed, had a primary obligation to "popularize" their subject among laymen in order to enable them to evaluate properly the facile, shallow, and ready-made opinions supplied in increasing quantities through the mass media of communication. Mrs. Parsons hoped that the pronouncers themselves might "be educated away from their conceits."

Perhaps the melancholy circumstances under which Mrs. Parsons' presidential address was delivered and the recency of her death when it was published in the *American Anthropologist* deterred expressions critical of her ideas. It would seem that at the time her ideas were presented, they might well have been open to criticism as inconsistent. Parsons believed that social commentators often erred, and even when no fault could be found in their opinions, danger lurked in the fact that their views were promulgated and absorbed on the basis of authority rather than reason. At the same time she warned anthropologists that they too ran the risk of being oracular rather than scientific. Yet, she argued strongly for the popularizing of anthropology as the means of bringing about a desirable intellectual "revolution." However, now that more than twenty years have elapsed since Elsie Parsons' death, it is possible to discern the concepts she was in the process of formulating but could not then set forth in precise and explicit terms. Applied anthropology, a new field in 1941 and the object of Mrs. Parsons' pointed criticism, as well as the even more recent development known as action anthropology, have been approaching what Mrs. Parsons apparently meant by the "popularization" of anthropology.

As early as 1941, anthropologists were free of the cultural blindness that led to the predictive errors of Alice Fletcher and the sense of personal affront experienced by Matilda Stevenson in viewing Zuñi acculturation. By then there was awareness that directed change must follow the course of voluntary change. That is, anthropologists knew that change must be congruent with the existing values and patterns of the group concerned, values and patterns to be discovered and defined by anthropologists. However, Elsie Clews Parsons' analogy of this type of anthropology to soothsaying was apt: the diviner is often exceedingly sensitive in manipulating observable social phenomena but cannot really read minds. During the last twenty years, practical utilizations of anthropology have been moving toward greater involvement and comprehension of the group served in the fact-finding and decision-making processes in the work of directed change. Ideally, the anthropologist endeavors to promote "a state of dynamic equilibrium within systems of human relationships," rather than to advance a particular program conceived of by well-intentioned and even well-informed outsiders as in the best interests of a society.[73] Elsie Clews Parsons' presidential address carries us to developments of the present in the history of women in the early years of anthropology.

Looking back over the careers of women from Smith to Parsons, it is possible to draw at least some tentative generalizations. Individual women have made specific contributions to the development of anthropology. However, the contributions of women as a group cannot be specified in comparison to contributions of men as a group. Some qualifications of these flat statements are, of course, in order and will be briefly considered, but fundamentally women have not confined themselves to the "female data" the fathers of anthropology and they themselves initially designated as their peculiar province. Even by the time the pronouncements were made, women had already branched out into other areas of investigation. Furthermore, albeit somewhat later, many prominent men in anthropology became associated with pioneer work in the intensive study of patterns of child care and training, nutrition, and other "female" data. The disbanding of the Women's Anthropological Society in 1899 was in itself a recognition of the universality of work carried out by the very first women anthropologists.

These generalizations should, however, be seen in the total social setting of American anthropology in its early years. It appears that it was not the exclusiveness, even reinforced by taboos, of male and female activities of "primitives" that suggested women might obtain data not readily disclosed to men, but the strong segregation of the sexes in Victorian society that produced the early anthropologists. Men were unwittingly reluctant to deal with matters in the field that were beneath their notice at home. Women broke the bonds of sexual ascription of ethnographic tasks, although they can hardly take credit for it. Women simply followed the dictates of their culture as unconsciously as men. Upper-class and even middle-class women of the latter half of the nineteenth century were expected to involve themselves with problems of social welfare and matters of religion, as well as to acquire an intelligent knowledge of local, national and world events. Business and politics lay in the hands of men, but women heard far more about these things than men knew about the details of domesticity. Furthermore, in a Victorian dwelling the isolation of individuals' activities by age, sex, and social status — let us not forget the "hired girl" — could not possibly occur in an earth lodge, tipi, or pueblo household. Women such as Fletcher, Smith, and Stevenson were brought up to learn from men and to listen to their views; thus in their field work they experienced little constraint in continuing to learn from male informants. Where these women exhibited a truly remarkable degree of adaptability was not with regard to sex-linked data, but in status-linked matters. Tibbles found it hard to believe that Alice Fletcher, a proper Bostonian, could accustom herself to the lack of privacy and physical hardships of life among the Plains Indians, and Tilly Stevenson herself admitted that until she visited the Zuñi she had no practical knowledge of so simple a task as washing clothes.

Women who did not conform to the norms of nineteenth-century society — and the point would apply to other periods as well — were either "bad women" or so intellectually gifted that, proverbial exceptions to the rule, they were accorded respect and egalitarian treatment by men. Women who succeeded were by definition notable for their intelligence and unconventional aspirations, but in most cases these traits were not enough, a fact to which Parsons was particularly sensitive. All of the women discussed had advantages of family wealth, social status, and an interest in education that allowed them greater latitude of behavior than if their families had been poor and ignorant. Nevertheless, limitations placed upon women did serve a useful selective function to the benefit of disciplines that they entered, although the strain imposed on individuals may have taken its toll in Stevenson's case and contributed to her feistiness. Clearly, gifted women were under far more pressure to prove themselves than were men so that the work of a surprising number of early women in anthropology was memorable. Even their mistakes, like the mistakes of early men important in the field, served to explore and mark dead-end avenues of investigation for the benefit of those who followed.

Although women were actually welcomed into anthropology because of an erroneous notion that they could and would be the only ones to obtain certain necessary information, the miscalculation worked to the advantage of women as individuals. They did not have to dissipate their energies in *fighting* for their rights but could apply them toward earning the esteem of their colleagues. On the other hand, the emphasis on the value of women in ethnological studies may have limited but certainly did not preclude their active participation in other branches of anthropology. Zelia Nuttall, for example, concentrated on archeology, and Alice Fletcher was interested in archeology long before she did ethnographic field work.[74] However, aside from some efforts to describe physical types of peoples studied, women who were pioneers in anthropology evinced no great inclination toward work in physical anthropology in either somatological or evolutionary terms. Since physical anthropology gained its major impetus from anatomists and medical men and remains a branch of anthropology having relatively few full-time practitioners, absence of women in the nineteenth century may be due to no more than statistical and occupational chance.[75]

With regard to the fields of anthropology with which most of the early women concerned themselves, unquestionably in particular instances the sex of the investigator helped or hindered her in obtaining certain types of data. Nevertheless, the fact of being a woman has been and continues to be but one of many personal variables, any one of which may figure most importantly in affecting the course of field work at different times and in various places. In addition to the individual traits of sex, age, training, personality structure, experience, and physical health and stamina, there were and are external variables influencing the amount and kind of information obtained. Among these may be listed the general political climate under which research is conducted, existing attitudes toward anthropologists and other outsiders, and the quality of interpersonal relationships among several coworkers.

Women in early American anthropology possessed in common only an exceptional amount of drive and sense of adventure to step beyond the place society reserved for the average woman. Even the personal lives of the six women discussed are dissimilar. Alice Fletcher and Frances Densmore never married; Zelia Nuttall was divorced; Matilda Stevenson was widowed at thirty-eight; and Erminnie Smith and Elsie Clews Parsons combined marriage and an anthropological career throughout their lives. However, having decided to become anthropologists, they virtually were obliged by their society to become outstanding anthropologists. Nevertheless, the problems they dealt with were influenced by the going theories and interests of their day and were not distinguished for any definably feminine characteristics. Contrary to their own opinion in 1885, there was really nothing in their "nature as women" that gave them "special adaptations" for the study of anthropology. Each brought her own unique nature and special adaptations as an individual to the study of anthropology.

Notes and References

1. This paper is exploratory rather than definitive. Collections of letters and other important manuscript materials were identified at the Peabody Museum, Harvard University, and the Archives of the Bureau of American Ethnology; but time limitations on this paper prevented me from consulting them. I hope that each subject may some day be accorded full-scale treatment, and that interest may be sparked to bring the existence of little-known biographical source material to the attention of anthropologists. In beginning my research I turned to various people who might direct me to source materials or who might have personal recollections of some of the women. In this regard, I wish to express my sincere thanks for the kind interest taken in my project by Professors Volney Jones and Leslie White, University of Michigan; Professor Arnold Pilling, Wayne State University, Detroit; the late Dr. A. V. Kidder, Sr. and Miss Margaret Currier, Harvard University; Professor A. I. Hallowell, University of Pennsylvania; Dr. Matthew W. Stirling, retired director of the Bureau of American Ethnology, of Washington, D. C.; Dr. William Sturtevant and Mrs. Margaret Blaker of the Bureau of American Ethnology; Dr. Clifford Evans, United States National Museum and Dr. Betty Meggers, Washington, D.C.; Dr. J. Alden Mason, Philadelphia; Mr. Ross Parmenter, New York; Dr. William N. Fenton, New York State Museum, Albany; the late Dr. S. A. Barrett, Berkeley, California; and Miss Mabel Densmore, Red Wing, Minnesota.

2. George Rosen, and Beate Caspari-Rosen, *400 Years of a Doctor's Life* (New York, 1947), pp. 87–92.

3. Rossiter Johnson (ed.), *Twentieth Century Biographical Dictionary of Notable Americans*, Boston, 1904; Vol. I, "Myra Colby Bradwell," n.p. Hereinafter cited as Johnson, 1904; Vol., ". . ."

4. Edward Lurie, *Louis Agassiz, A Life in Science* (Chicago, 1960), pp. 166–67, 200–01, 380–81. Acceptance of women in the various sciences was not unique to the United States in the nineteenth century; *cf.* Alexander F. Chamberlain, "Johanna Mestorf" (obituary), *American Anthropologist,* Vol. XI, No. 3; 536–37. The career of this German archeologist, 1829–1909, included curatorial and professorial appointments.

5. Whether the American Association for the Advancement of Science ever discriminated against women or whether it was simply a good platform for arguing women's rights is difficult to determine, but in 1880 an impassioned feminist plea was entered in a paper by Ellen Hardin Walworth under Natural History — not Anthropology, entitled, "Field Work By Amateurs," A.A.A.S. *Proceedings*, XXXIX, 597–602.

6. Edward B. Tylor, "How The Problems of American Anthropology Present Themselves to the English Mind," Anthropological Society of Washington, *Transactions*, Vol. III, 1885, 81–95 (quotation on 93). The address was first printed in *Science*, IV (1884), 545–51.

7. W. H. Holmes, "Matilda Coxe Stevenson" (obituary), *American Anthropologist*, Vol. 18, No. 3, 1916, 552–59. Hereinafter cited as Holmes, 1916. Holmes designates Stevenson the founder of the Women's Anthropological Society, 555.

8. Daniel S. Lamb, "The Story of The Anthropological Society of Washington," *American Anthropologist*, VIII (1906), 564–579. Lamb provides the sequence and details noted regarding the joint meetings between the A.S.W. and W.A.S. that led to the eventual disbanding of the women's group, but does not discuss the Sanitary Improvement Company.

9. I am indebted to Dr. Evans and to Dr. Meggers for providing information concerning the Sanitary Improvement Company and making available to me the pamphlet regarding the W.A.S. as well as drawing my attention to George M. Kober, *The History and Development of the Housing Movement in the City of Washington, D.C.*, Washington, D.C.: Washington Sanitary Housing Companies (1927), p. 10, which details the work of Miss Clara de Gaffenried.

10. *Transactions of the American Ethnological Society*, I (New York, 1845), *passim*, sets forth information regarding the constitution and organization and a list of charter members.

11. *Congrès International des Americanistes Compte-Rendu de la Huitème Session Tenue a Paris en 1890*, Paris, 1892, 11, 13.

12. Alice Fletcher, *A Letter From The World's Industrial Exposition at New Orleans, To The Various Indian Tribes Who Are Interested in Education* (Carlisle, Pa. [1883]), 4 pp.

13. W. H. Holmes, "The World's Fair Congress of Anthropology," in *Selected Papers from the American Anthropologist, 1888–1920*, ed. Frederica de Laguna (Evanston, Ill., 1960), pp. 423–34. Five of the 38 participants listed by Holmes were women.

14. Holmes, 1916, 554.

15. Alfred M. Tozzer, "Zelia Nuttall" (obituary), *American Anthropologist*, XXXV (1933), 475–82. Hereinafter cited as Tozzer, 1933.

16. Johnson, 1904, Vol. X, "Erminnie Smith." In reply to my letter, William N. Fenton reported having read at the Bureau of American Ethnology the correspondence of Erminnie Smith, "a wonderful letter writer," to Major Powell; Fenton also notes the existence of correspondence between Smith and Fletcher. He considers Smith to have been a good linguist and a "much better scientist than Harriet Maxwell Converse" who also did early work in Iroquois folklore.

17. Johnson, 1904, Vol. X, "Erminnie Smith."

18. An abstract of Smith's paper on jade appears in A.A.A.S. *Proceedings*, XXVIII (1879), 523–25. Thus far, the location of the entire paper remains unknown.

19. A.A.A.S. *Proceedings*, XXX (1880); abstracts of "Comparative Differences in the Iroquois Group of Dialects," 315–19, and "Animal Myths," 321–23.

20. Johnson, 1904, Vol. X, "Erminnie Smith."

21. A.A.A.S. *Proceedings*, XXXII (1882); Smith, 402–03, 595; Fletcher, 580–84, 595; Bowers, 595.

22. *Science*, V (1885), 3–4.

23. See, "Report of the Director," Smithsonian Institution, Bureau of Ethnology, *Annual Reports*, I–VII (1879–1885). VII, xxxi, notes Smith's death and continuation of her work by J. N. B. Hewitt; Vol. II, 47–166 contains Smith's "Myths of the Iroquois": with illustrations of the stories apparently done by an Iroquois informant.

24. John R. Swanton, "John Napoleon Brinton Hewitt" (obituary), *American Anthropologist*, XL (1938), 286–90.

25. Walter Hough, "Alice Cunningham Fletcher" (obituary), *American Anthropologist*, XXV (1923), 254–58. Hereinafter cited as Hough,

1923. Hough notes that Fletcher was actively interested in the work of the Peabody as early as 1880 or 1881 but was not officially listed among the personnel until 1886. She was instrumental in the preservation of the Serpent Mound in Ohio and her first scientific interest in anthropology was as much archeological as ethnological.

26. Among the many benevolent groups interested in the welfare of the American Indian was the "Mohonk Conference" founded in 1882 by a philanthropist, Albert K. Smiley, who opened his estate, now a summer resort, at Lake Mohonk to visitors who gathered each year to discuss Indian problems. The group was not a society and had no regular membership but the U.S. Board of Indian Commissioners, a semiofficial investigative body under the Indian Bureau made up primarily of interested private citizens, often met with the conference and held special sessions at Mohonk. The conferences continued more than three decades, and well into the twentieth century, with cooperating organizations, clung to the ideals of individual enterprise and assimilation of the Indian. Among the cooperating groups were the Society of American Indians and the Women's National Indian Association. See *The Quarterly Journal of the Society of American Indians*, II (1914), 172–74; and "Mohonk Platform of Principles, adopted by the Mohonk Conference, October 9, 1885," *Publications of the Women's National Indian Association*, pamphlet, 4 pp., no date, no site.

Fletcher was a primary force in these organizations and, in the present day, it seems incredible that she could have been imbued with ideas of using force to get Indian children educated, spending as quickly as possible any capital held by tribes, and reducing tribal lands. The nine points set forth in the 1885 Mohonk Platform are understandable to some extent only if it is recalled that in the 1870's and 1880's Indian reservations were, in effect, prison camps designed to keep "hostile savages" in control. Kindly whites, guilty in the realization that the Indian had been misused, sought to grant human dignity and rights of citizenship to Indians although their methods were drastic and threatened the Indians' only remaining source of security, community life. The almost religious fervor concerning the sacredness of private property is a most notable feature of these groups.

27. Alice Fletcher, "The Hako: A Pawnee Ceremony," Smithsonian Institution, Bureau of American Ethnology, *Annual Report*, XXI (1904–1905). A complete bibliography of Fletcher's scholarly works accom-

panies the Hough obituary.

28. Charles F. Lummis, "In Memoriam, Alice C. Fletcher," *Art and Archeology*, XV (1923). See also "Alice C. Fletcher Memorial Meeting," *El Palacio*, XVI (1923), 83–88, which discusses Fletcher's remarkable powers of gentle persuasion, work in behalf of education in American archeology, and her "practical" approach to Indian problems.

29. Paul Radin, personal conversation with N.O.L., 1958. This impatient dismissal of my casual inquiry whether he had known Alice Fletcher distressed me at the time. I simply wished to know more about the woman who did field work on the Plains before the echoes of Little Big Horn had barely ceased reverberating and the hostilities of the Ghost Dance of 1890 were yet to come. On the basis of the present research, Radin's reaction is entirely understandable. With almost anyone else Fletcher could be all sweet reasonableness as the "expert" on Indian policy, but Radin was one of the few people in the early 1900's who actually saw what was happening to her beloved Omaha and other tribes. He was probably at no pains in Fletcher's presence to conceal *his* opinions based on a great deal more scholarly objectivity than Fletcher's emotional commitment to the allotment system.

30. Thomas Henry Tibbles, *Buckskin and Blanket Days* (New York, 1957). Hereinafter cited as Tibbles (1957). The item noted occurs on p. 236. Tibble's manuscript was actually written in 1905, but additional materials were gathered by the publishers, including a biography of Tibbles, for the 1957 publication.

31. Tibbles (1957), p. 261. Pages 268–70 recount one argument Fletcher lost although she won the day. Tibbles was terribly distressed that Fletcher's outspoken criticism of Indian policy and questioning of Indians about injustices would get the party into trouble and even land them in prison — he had had experience with the amazing power wielded by Indian agents on the frontier. What really exasperated Tibbles, however, was Fletcher's combination of foolhardy crusader's zeal and insistence on the proprieties of cultured society. "Quoth our Boston dame to me, 'The House is the proper place for the agent to receive a lady.'" She was finally prevailed upon to visit the Rosebud Reservation Agent at his office and to Tibbles' relief opened conversation politely with a pleasantry about the weather; but Tibbles' heart sank when the agent, obviously considering the party nothing but nosey busy-bodies remarked, "I regulate everything here but the weather." Fletcher chose to consider this

a lighthearted witticism — she had an ace up her sleeve. She presented her official credentials and the agent wilted as she knew he would.

32. Tibbles (1957), p. 260.

33. Francis La Flesche, "Alice C. Fletcher" (obituary), *Science*, LVII (August 17, 1923), 115. Hereinafter cited as La Flesche, 1923.

34. La Flesche (1923), 115.

35. La Flesche (1923), 115–16; Tibbles (1957), 295. Tibbles takes full credit for the Dawes Severalty Act. Actually, experiments of the Indian Bureau in granting patents in fee to individual Indians and gifts of land for family homesteads by benevolent groups were the model on which Fletcher's views and the Dawes Act were based.

36. Alice Fletcher and Francis La Flesche, "The Omaha Tribe," Smithsonian Institution, Bureau of American Ethnology, *Annual Report*, XXVII (1905–1906), 640–42. Actual publication of the *Reports* lags behind the sequence of volume dates so that information collected in 1910 was included at the end of this volume. Fletcher's assessments are given on pp. 640–42; comparisons are derived from my own observations of Nebraska Winnebago and Omaha, 1950 and 1954, and discussions with Omaha people at the American Indian Chicago Conference, June 13–20, 1961, as well as from Mead (*See* n. 37).

37. Margaret Mead, *The Changing Culture of An Indian Tribe* (New York, 1932), p. 51. It is striking that while Mead's study shows the effects of tremendous changes between 1882 and 1930, particularly from *ca.* 1910, some thirty years later her descriptions of life among the Omaha in 1930 are still generally applicable.

38. *Cf.* Harold C. Fey and D'Arcy McNickle, *Indians and Other Americans* (New York, 1959), pp. 72–79, for an historical analysis of the Dawes Severalty Act and statistics on land losses.

39. Tibbles (1957), pp. 278–79.

40. Alice Fletcher, "Music As Found in Certain North American Indian Tribes," *Music Review* (August, 1893), 534–38. Quotations from first and final pages of article.

41. In 1946 when I was a young graduate student at the University of Chicago, well indoctrinated in the importance of rapport and empathy and had even had some field experience, I attended a lecture by Paul Radin and was outraged at his matter-of-fact account of obtaining certain data by means of psychological and economic pressures. In later years,

when Radin and I became friends and even worked together, I was able to understand somewhat better the sense of urgency that motivated early field workers to obtain data by almost any means that would not actually skew the information or cause the anthropologist to be ousted from the group. In truth, some data would have been irrevocably lost but for the work of Radin and others. However, the wounds still smarting as a result of Radin's methods did not simplify my first field work among the traditionalist Winnebago.

42. La Flesche (1923), 116, recounts a traditional ceremony held specially as an expression of thanks to Fletcher for her work in behalf of the Omaha. At the close, the leader "told Miss Fletcher that she was free to study this and any other tribal rites."

43. Hough (1923), 254–55.

44. Holmes (1916), 557–59.

45. Holmes (1916), 552–56.

46. Matilda C. Stevenson, "The Zuni Indians: Their Mythological, Esoteric Societies and Ceremonies," Smithsonian Institution, Bureau of American Ethnology, *Annual Report,* XXIII (1901–1902), 310, 380. Hereinafter cited as Stevenson (1901–1902).

47. Holmes (1916), 553.

48. Holmes (1916), 558–59 lists Stevenson's bibliography.

49. Stevenson (1901–1902), 17.

50. J. Walter Fewkes, "Contributions to Hopi History, 1890 — II. Oraibi in 1890." *American Anthropologist,* XXII (1922), 268–83. Kiva incident and quotation, 273.

51. I am indebted to William Sturtevant for his kindness in drawing my attention to both the article and illustration from the *Illustrated Police News* and for providing me with copies. Dr. Sturtevant brought the first draft of this paper to the attention of Dr. Stirling who wrote his comments to Dr. Sturtevant in a letter, December 21, 1964. Dr. Stirling has kindly granted permission to cite the letter, and all references to Stirling in the text derive from his letter.

52. Stevenson (1901–1902), 379; 381–82.

53. Stevenson (1901–1902), 608. Fenton's letter already referred to includes some of the Stevenson legends and sources of further data which unfortunately could not be consulted before the deadline date on the present paper. Like other people who recalled stories of her ter-

rible temper, Fenton notes "Tilly's fights with Major Powell who used to fire her regularly and then she would threaten to invoke Congress on him and get herself restored to office. On one of these occasions, he got so mad he had a stroke and that finished him." Stirling's letter substantiates this account as he learned it from May S. Clark, who was present in Powell's office; ". . . Tilly stormed in the door, leaned over Powell's desk and shaking her finger in his face, shouted, 'Major Powell, you are a damned liar!' The major, face flushed, rose in his chair and fell back with the first of the strokes which later resulted in his death." Stirling substantiated another incident first mentioned to me by Fenton: once when Stevenson was asked to itemize an expense account, she filed under informants' fees, "One man, one night, one dollar." On another occasion, according to Stirling:

> *She included a case of Scotch in her expense account, which of course was turned down. She insisted that it was necessary in her work, since nothing else would induce the Indians to give out their more secret information. It was pointed out to her that it was illegal to give whiskey to Indians. She replied that it was only illegal to sell it to them. The item became a matter of pride and principle with her, and she insisted she would fight it through.*

Harry Dorsey, administrative assistant to the Secretary (who told me this story), finally settled the matter by paying her from the Smithsonian Institution private funds, but allowing her to think she had won her point, and that it had gone through the Government Accounting Office."

54. A. V. Kidder, Sr., personal correspondence with N.O.L. Stirling commenting on this paper, notes: "J. P. Harrington also told me the story of Tilly's Indian name. He said that the Indians told her it meant "Little Mother" and that she was quite proud of it: Actually, the literal translation of the name was 'Big broad buttocks like a mesa.' "

55. Tozzer (1933), 475–82. Unless otherwise cited, all biographical data on Zelia Nuttall are taken from this source which also includes a full listing of her bibliography.

56. XXVII (1928), 40–43.

57. "Frances Densmore," *Science*, CXXV (1957), 1240. Hereinafter cited as "Densmore," *Science* (1957). Just as this article in honor of

Densmore's ninetieth birthday went to press, news was received of her death.

58. Phyliss Ashmun, "Indian Music Expert Reveals Highlights of Fascinating Career," *Ashland Daily Press* (Ashland, Wisconsin), July 28, 1945. Hereinafter cited as Ashmun, 1945. Densmore was seventy-eight years old at the time of this interview and was engaged in a study of Indian music in the Upper Peninsula of Michigan for the University of Michigan.

59. Stirling letter, December 21, 1964. For further data on Densmore's work with the Bureau of American Ethnology, *cf.* "Densmore," *Science* (1957); Marquis, *Who Was Who*, III (Chicago, 1960), 222.

60. Ashmun, 1945.

61. Mabel Densmore, personal correspondence with N.O.L.

62. Frances Densmore, "Chippewa Music," Smithsonian Institution, Bureau of American Ethnology, *Bulletin 45* (1910), 3. The second volume of this work appeared as *Bulletin 53* (1913).

63. Frances Densmore, "The Music of the Filipinos," *American Anthropologist*, VIII (1906), 611–32.

64. "Densmore," *Science* (1957).

65. Ashmun, 1945.

66. A. A. Kroeber, "Elsie Clews Parsons" (obituary, Part II of two parts), *American Anthropologist*, XLV (1943), 252–55. The first three pages detail biographical data on birth, marriage, etc.

67. Leslie Spier, "Elsie Clews Parsons" (obituary, Part I), *American Anthropologist*, XLV (1943), 244–51. Hereinafter cited as Spier (1943). Assessment of Parson's sociological writing, 245–47.

68. Spier (1943), 245–50.

69. Gladys Reichard, "Elsie Clews Parsons," *Journal of American Folklore*," Vol. LVI (1943), 45–48. (Parsons' bibliography, 48–56.) Hereinafter cited as Reichard (1943). This entire issue of the *JAF* is a memorial in honor of Parsons.

70. Spier (1943), 244.

71. Reichard (1943), 48.

72. "Anthropology and Prediction," *American Anthropologist*, XLIV (1942), 337–44.

73. "Code of Ethics of The Society for Applied Anthropology" (Mimeograph, 7 pp. including discussion of Code by John W. Bennett, 1962, 2–7).

74. A. I. Hallowell, "The Beginnings of Anthropology in America," *Selected Papers from The American Anthropologist, 1888–1920,* ed. Frederica de Laguna (Evanston, 1960), pp. 1–90. Fletcher is noted here only for her archeological interests in her work with F. W. Putnam in raising money to purchase the Serpent Mound area and turning title over to the Ohio Archeological and Historical Society in 1900. See Hough (1923), 254–58 for further discussion of Fletcher's interest in archeology.

75. That women were not oblivious to the problems of physical anthropology may be seen in Alice Fletcher, "The Problems of The Unity or The Plurality and The Probable Place of Origin of The American Aborigines. (A Symposium.) Some Ethnological Aspects of the Problem," *American Anthropologist,* XVI (1912), 37–39.